DRIVEN
—TO—
DISCIPLESHIP

**Discovering God's Love
for You and for Others**

DRIVEN
—TO—
DISCIPLESHIP

Discovering God's Love
for You and for Others

Jeff Henderson

Published in the United States of America by Credo House Publishers,
a division of Credo Communications LLC, Grand Rapids, Michigan
credohousepublishers.com

Unless otherwise indicated, Scripture quotations are from the HOLY BIBLE, NEW
INTERNATIONAL VERSION®. NIV®. Copyright © 1973, 1978, 1984 by International
Bible Society. Used by permission of Zondervan. All rights reserved.

ISBN: 978-1-62586-272-3

Cover design by Alex Henderson
Interior design by Believe Book Design LLC
Editing by Donna Huisjen

Printed in the United States of America
First Edition

Then Jesus came to them and said, "All authority in heaven and on earth has been given to me. Therefore go and make disciples of all nations, baptizing them in the name of the Father and of the Son, and the Holy Spirit, and teaching them to obey everything I have commanded you."

Matthew 28:18–20

"The sovereign LORD has given me a well-instructed tongue, to know the word that sustains the weary. He wakens me morning by morning, wakens my ear to listen like one being instructed. The Sovereign LORD has opened my ears; I have not been rebellious, I have not turned away."

Isaiah 50:4–5

Contents

Foreword

This is a book that speaks from Jeff's heart to anyone who is ready to hear God's heart being offered, breath after breath. Each encounter shows the love of God offered to many different persons, offering hope and encouragement without judgment. The words come from a man with a background of an athlete, a husband, a father, a teacher, a coach, a Christian leader and warrior, and a faithful friend who speaks from a place of vulnerability and experience that he offers to his readers with no strings attached. Everyone is invited to receive the vast love of God.

Enjoy the journey with him.

Loren Siffring
friend and mentor

Preface

Purpose. All people search for purpose, for meaning. I believe our purpose, our meaning, is right in front of our noses. God is extremely interested in the joy and fulfillment of our lives. As Irenaeus, the early church leader was quoted as stating, "The glory of God is man fully alive." This is obviously "man" being inclusive of men and women. God delights in our purpose fulfilled, our hearts on fire for his purposes and plans. And, he has made his plans and purpose clear in the words of scripture that we have to affirm the will of God.

My hope and prayer are that you can see more clearly the beautiful, simple plans the Lord has for you as you are driven to the discipleship path for yourself and others.

Thanks!

I want to express my deepest thanks and gratitude to the following friends for their partnership in seeing this book come to fruition: Keith and Janell, Tony and Dawn, Mike and Sharon. Your help and support have seen this project through and without you, would not have taken place. I praise God for you and your faithfulness in friendship, counsel, and ministry!

Part One

Being a Disciple:
Following the Master, Jesus the Messiah

Chapter 1

To Be Called

 My son wants to kill himself . . . I don't know what to do . . . Can you help?"

This is how it all began.

My phone buzzed in my pocket around 9:00 p.m. After a day of teaching middle school English and coaching wrestling after school, I was feeling it. I was tired. I knew the end of the evening was drawing close as I sat in my family room, warm and cozy, watching a TV show with my wife and daughter, something we did on most nights before turning in. I knew that a 5:00 a.m. wake-up and workout were looming large for the morning.

Yet I saw the name on the phone and recognized it as that of a new acquaintance through church; so, I answered, knowing this might entail several minutes of questions and answers. His first words were, "My son wants to kill himself . . . I don't know what to do . . . Can you help? You are the only one I could think of to call."

That was the last thing I thought I would hear. I replied that I would be over as soon as I could and asked him to text me the address. I told Anne, my wife, that a family had a desperate need, and she gave me her understanding nod as I grabbed my jacket and headed out the door. It was a short drive, and I prayed during the ten minutes of time I had: "Father, you know the circumstances. You have the answers. Holy Spirit, help me to listen to you as I listen to them. Give me wisdom and tenderness with your authority over the powers of darkness that are lying to this young man. Allow a breakthrough that brings healing and wholeness to him and his family. Thank you, Holy Spirit, for going ahead of me and filling that room, that house, and for leading the way. I will wait on you. In Jesus's name. Amen."

Somehow, all at once, I knew the path—the progression that would most likely need to take place. No matter what we discussed, I knew inside that we needed to find professional help right away, and I knew where we should go.

My GPS guided me to the address. As I pulled up to the house, the friend who had called met me at the door. I could see his wife pacing back and forth in the house through a window. As I met him, I gave him a hug, noticing the desperate look on his face, which was a pasty white color at this point. He frantically spat out the circumstances that had brought the family to this place. We walked inside, and he continued to brief me on the details. I politely asked him to give me some time with his son, who was sitting on the couch.

I knew this young man from school, although it had been several years since I had last seen him. I asked if I could sit down next to him and talk, and he nodded his head up and down slowly as a yes. His head was down and his long hair draped over his eyes, which were sullen. He looked as if he had given up all hope. In a weakened yet articulate voice, he began to state over and over again how much of a failure he had been. He explained, in a somewhat disjointed manner, that he had come home smelling of marijuana. He said he had denied this to his parents at first, but his dad had found items in his room that confirmed his use.

He was caught. That was the last straw in his mind. He had let down his family and his friends. His girlfriend had left him for the same reason—his pot use and failures—and now he was done. He had lost his job as well, in a string of several others he had also lost recently. At twenty-two years old he felt defeated in every way. He added that he was a loser, overweight, and depressed and that all he wanted to do was go to his room, consume the bottle of pills he had reserved for this occasion, and die.

I quietly sat next to this broken young man, as I listened and waited, praying silently for God's wisdom and direction. Sensing what I needed to do, without a word I wrapped my arm around this large youngster and pulled him close. He hung his head, leaning into my shoulder, and began to weep, first a little and then with heavy sobs. I felt his warm tears fall onto my sweater. At this point his parents stopped their pacing and also began to weep.

I could sense the Spirit of God moving in the room. After several minutes I asked David (name changed for the purpose of anonymity) if it would be okay if we spoke. He nodded in the affirmative as he wiped his eyes and sat up a bit straighter. I looked at him. What I saw was a young man broken by his decisions and mistaken direction. He was realizing the weight of his actions.

I began, with a gentle yet confident tone, "David, when I last knew you as a student in school, you were filled with energy and purpose. What happened?" He began to explain that, after graduating from high school and starting to work, he had sensed depression coming on from time to time. He missed his friends but, feeling alone, did not share these emotions with his family. He was afraid to open up and began to use marijuana as an escape. He described staying home from work, driving his car around town, getting high, and beginning to eat more and more to try to medicate himself from the continual depressing thoughts.

After he had lost another job, his girlfriend broke up with him because he wouldn't change and was only getting worse. David knew this was true, so, after an evening of depression and pot, he came home, found the pills he thought would do the trick, and went to his room to end his misery. That's when his parents confronted him. That's when he admitted everything. That's when they called me. And here we were, the family experiencing an outflow of fresh tears, fresh feelings of hopelessness, and fresh discouragement, as seen in his eyes and on his parents' faces . . . yet I knew there was direction, a path, and hope and prayed he would be open to them.

I affirmed his feelings of hopelessness, reiterating aloud the circumstances he had expressed. However, I shared another understanding, another point of view. I explained what God's view of him was and is. God sees him with delight, purpose, and hope for his future. When he questioned this, I related that the Lord created each of us in his own image, with destiny, ability, and vision for what we can do and what we can become. I shared examples of how God has taken so many from broken decisions and hopelessness (citing individuals such as Moses, Peter, Saul of Tarsus, and myself) and shown each one that he is the God of breakthroughs. He makes a way where there seems to be no way.

"What you are going through, David, is no small thing. It is huge, and you are at a point where you see the hopelessness of your life and decisions—without God. The truth is that he designed you for his purposes, for a life that has value, and he can get you there. You simply have to begin to trust enough to ask him to renew you—your mind, your heart, your life. Give him the chance tonight to lead you."

"How do I do that?" David asked sincerely.

"David," I responded gently, "trust the direction I am going to suggest to you and your family."

"What do I need to do?" David asked cautiously, with a bit of uneasiness in his voice.

"First of all, would you be willing to give me the pills you spoke about?" David hesitated, then slowly reached into his coat pocket, brought them out, and handed them to me. "Do you have any others?" I asked. He was emphatic that those were the only ones.

"Next," I said, "is the need for you to get help . . . to get your thinking straightened out. You have been battling this for a long time, right?" He nodded in response. "You have trusted me this far, so I would like you to trust me again. I know a place nearby that is warm and understanding with people who, like you, are dealing with depression and thoughts of taking their own lives. They can help."

David was hesitant. "I have to go tonight?"

"Yes, I think that would be a really important step right now—while this is fresh. The thoughts you have had are still in there, so the sooner we get you help—people who love you and are trained in what you're struggling with—the sooner you can start on a better path that leads to your getting healthy again."

I braced myself for more resistance, but, amazingly, he yielded and asked what he needed. By this time it was nearing midnight. I asked him to pack a few things for a few days and assured him that I would explain more on the way. Before he went to his room, he allowed me to pray with him, and his family joined us. We prayed over David that he would know the love of Jesus Christ for himself personally and that he would once again see the Lord as the rescuer, the Father he truly is. We prayed for guidance and open doors to follow with every step.

When he went to his room, his younger brother, who had been in the house listening from a distance, said that he would help David. He put his arm around him, and they went upstairs. David's parents at that point had several questions. "What was the place? How long might it be? What would happen? Would this work?"

I calmly explained that there was a program nearby that specialized in young adults with suicidal thoughts. I had been there on several occasions with teens from our church youth group and other young adults who needed help—and each one was helped and given a new perspective and direction. My friend looked at me and began to weep again as he asked, "I don't know how to do this . . . Will you go with us and help us?"

"Of course," I replied reassuringly. "I will be with you every step of the way." When David returned, we left. David rode with me and his parents drove together in their car.

The rest of the night entailed a series of steps through an intake process, paperwork, evaluations, and David being admitted for help. When David was finally on his way to his room, accompanied by a nurse and a young man who served as a counselor, David's parents walked with me to the parking garage. They thanked me through tired, swollen eyes, and I asked them to keep me in the loop as to what was happening with their son.

As I got into my car, I checked the time. "Well," I thought to myself, I don't think I will get up for that workout now." The thought was somewhat amusing to me, as I exhaled and breathed a prayer of thanks: "Lord, you alone can make a way for this boy tonight. Thank you, thank you. Get him through this, Lord—get him to a new place where he wants to live and can recognize your hand on his life. Heal him and heal his family. Thank you, Father."

Now, several years later, David is alive and well, although I haven't seen him in a while. What mattered is that David and his family could call and could trust that God had an answer to their need. I believe this is the heart cry of many, many people: "Lord, I don't know what to do . . . I am lost in this situation. Lord, please help!"

Psalm 10 identifies for me the cry many of us have uttered at different points. Verse 1 pleads, "Why, Lord, do you stand far off? Why do you hide yourself in times of trouble?" This was the excruciating, gut-level question from David the psalmist as he watched ungodliness reign with no foreseeable answer in sight, . . . until he considered the time ahead and God's faithfulness to one day answer his prayer. He writes in verse 14: "But you, God, see the trouble of the afflicted; you consider their grief and take it in hand. The victims commit themselves to you; you are the helper of the fatherless."

There are those who at this moment are at the place of verse one—crying out. In response to their cries, God taps the hearts of his children, nudging them to respond and to walk alongside those who are praying for his help. They receive *from* him *through* us, disciples who long to be used in his kingdom for his purposes.

How do we get to the place where we are disciples of the Lord Jesus Christ who have become disciple-makers, leading others to Jesus through any and every situation imaginable? It all begins with wanting to walk with Jesus Christ, to be his disciple.

Chapter 2

To Be a Disciple

To be a disciple. What does that mean? What was Jesus saying, truly, when in Matthew 28 he declared so strongly to his disciples, "All authority in heaven and on earth has been given to me. *Therefore go and make disciples of all nations, baptizing them* in the name of the Father and of the Son and of the Holy Spirit, and *teaching them to obey* everything I have commanded you. And surely *I am with you* always, to the very end of the age" (emphases added)?

It seems apparent that Jesus was sending his followers with the directive, "go." He also made simple and clear the goal behind the going: "make disciples." We know that a disciple is not a part-time Christian. Discipleship entails all-in, full-time allegiance to Jesus Christ. Our examples as Christ's followers are the early disciples, and specifically those twelve who walked with Jesus wherever he went, completely on his schedule, according to his plans and not their own. Our model, as theirs, is Jesus. He led, he taught, and they followed. Okay, not quite perfectly, but they followed! They learned, they stumbled, and they grew bit by bit with their eyes on and their trust in Jesus.

What was it like when you first came to Jesus and started to follow him? What led you to the reality that you wanted to follow Jesus Christ? What were you like before that decision, and what happened in your heart, mind, and life afterward? That, my friend, is your testimony. It is the testimony of someone who was changed by the love and power of God's resurrected Son, Jesus Christ. That is the story of how you became a disciple. The "why" of your following is now the central issue; your story is your testimony of becoming a disciple.

Here is my story of becoming a disciple.

1981. It was March, a fresh new springtime with sunny, slightly warmer Michigan weather. My third college wrestling season had ended, although not nearly as I had hoped it would, and I was searching. While I had become a college All-American the year before, the 1981 season had been filled with injuries and lost hopes.

In contrast, my new roommate, who happened to be my wrestling teammate, Dorr, was living a purpose-filled life as a college junior, walking with a solid disposition, which made me curious; it appealed to me, especially with my bruised feelings for how the past season had ended.

Dorr and I, as college sophomores, had both placed sixth in the previous national championships. As we descended the podium and looked at what we had just accomplished, however, we both found it unsatisfying. We wanted more! We decided then and there to room together the next year and push each other toward being on the top of the podium. Nothing else would do.

School progressed, and we talked more and more about the possibilities of the next season before moving back to our parents' homes for summer break. After the summer we merged at our apartment, ready to train and push ourselves to new levels. However, something was different about my new roommate. He seemed more confident and purposeful. He said he would no longer attend parties, indulge in drinking, or the like. Not that he or I had been "partiers," by any stretch, but he made it known that there would be no alcohol in our apartment.

Wow—pretty big standard for college students. "What is this all about?" I wondered out loud. Dorr explained to me that he had grown up in a Christian family and that, while in college, he had more or less lived apart from the faith he had been taught. As he explained to me, during the past summer he had worked as a counselor at a Christian camp and had made some decisions, among them that he had "rededicated" his life to Jesus Christ. My response was something like, "We are Americans, so we're all Christians, right?" Dorr smiled and responded, "No, we are not all Christians because we were born in America. That's a personal decision. There's a lot to explain, and you will just have to watch and see what is different." That made me curious . . .

As I was growing up, a few things had planted seeds in my life and set an example of following Jesus. My sister Pam had decided to get baptized when she was a teenager. I remember her solid stance and decision to be baptized, solidifying her intention to follow Christ. I wish I had understood more but did not at that time, beyond the image of what that had meant to her.

My best friend in high school, Jeff Williams, had decided to follow Christ at a Billy Graham Crusade. He had been very consistent in sharing Bible verses with me, and that had started to make a dent in my thinking. My family attended church periodically, and whenever the hymn "Holy, Holy, Holy" was played on the pipe organ with the choirs singing, I sensed something special. These recollections may have been the very seeds that were stirred by my roommate's newfound faith.

I was the average college student. I'd wake up every morning, leave my bed unkempt, stumble into the kitchen, and make some coffee. After the coffee had cleared the cobwebs, I would decide what to do and either procrastinate a while longer or get busy studying and get ready for class. Dorr, on the other hand, was up at the first light. He read his Bible and also read through another binder that I would later discover contained a list of people and things he was praying about. Yep, my name was in there as one he was praying for. I knew that because one morning I picked up the binder to look and discovered my name on his prayer list.

When the wrestling season began, I noticed a new fire in Dorr's workouts. He never complained, never weaseled his way out of a challenge, and was brutal. Although I was lighter in weight and not one of his main workout partners, there were a few occasions when I would have to practice with him. I definitely noticed the intensity and ferocity he wrestled with in those practices.

After one such practice I asked him, "Why do you practice like such a beast? I don't think most guys will want to continue to practice with you at the pace you're going." I will never forget his response, as he boldly stated, "If Jesus Christ can carry a cross for me, then I can give him my wrestling practice." I was stunned. Dorr had just brought Jesus into the practice room. It hit me like an arrow to the chest. I understood a little bit more of what the power and life of Jesus looks like in a man.

I could not deny the reality of the change in my roommate. While Dorr never came out and asked me questions or spoke with me about Jesus or Christianity directly, I wondered where he was getting this newfound integrity and grit. I wanted a Bible so I could check this thing out for myself. Finally, one day I summoned up the courage and asked Dorr for a Bible. Shortly after that he gave me a Bible, which I began to read, beginning in Genesis. I continued that habit for a while looking for something, but really, I didn't know what.

I spent several months with many failed attempts at reading Genesis and making deals with God, which was my simple misunderstanding based on failing to realize that God was not looking for a "deal." He was allowing me to see how flawed my thinking was about him and how afraid I was of taking further steps in this faith I was learning about.

To add to this, my wrestling coach, Jim Scott, gave me a small book about priorities, centered around the life of Christ. This, too, added to my understanding of the purpose of Jesus's life, death, and resurrection. It took me several months of wandering and wondering: wandering spiritually, searching but not satisfied with my vacillating thoughts about faith, and wondering about the new ideas I was learning while reading the Bible my roommate had given me.

The wrestling season had ended, this time for me with injuries and disappointments and no podium. I was frustrated, disappointed, and feeling lonely. Finally, one morning I was up early, thinking about going for a run but also interested in partying because that was a somewhat new adventure. I had taken up drinking and using marijuana occasionally with some friends. While I knew this wasn't good for me from an athletic standpoint, it took my mind off the more pressing issue before me: What about Jesus? What about what the Bible was saying about his life and death and resurrection? What about me? Where did I stand with all of it?

I stepped outside to decide which direction I would take and elected to party. However, I was sorely dissatisfied with my own decision. After a few minutes of indecisiveness, I went back to my apartment to go for that run I had thought about earlier. I went into my bedroom to find my running gear, and Dorr followed me into the room. Somehow, he must have figured out what I had been up to, and I could tell that he wanted to say something to me.

It was then that I noticed tears in his eyes. *He is crying*, I thought incredulously, *about me!* That realization stopped me in my tracks. I don't know if anyone had ever before shown me that kind of care—crying because of me, caring about my life. Dorr looked up from the floor at which he had been staring and asked me in a saddened voice, "Jeff, is there anything you are doing that is getting you closer to God?"

Then, lowering his head once again, he walked out of the room. I don't quite know how to explain it, but at that moment I suddenly knew what he meant. A light turned on inside me. I said to myself something like, *Yeah, what am I doing? Why am I playing around with this decision and not stepping up and making it? I now know the truth—I've read how Jesus Christ went to the cross for me—for me! What do I have ahead of me? Total uncertainty about life and my future. I know God promises he will walk me through life and that he holds the future. I don't know what the future holds, but I do know that he is good, and I am going to trust him.*

It seemed as though a posture of humility was moving inside me. I knew this was a significant decision, so I knelt on the floor . . . Then I placed my head on the carpet and prayed something like, "God, I *know* I am a sinner. I have been incredibly selfish. You know the list of my sins, which seems endless. I know you died for me. I know you are alive. Please forgive me. Come into my life, and, whatever you put inside my roommate to make him strong in his faith, put that in me, too!"

I stayed in that position for a moment, assessing my thoughts and realizing that I had just made an all-in decision to follow Jesus Christ. Suddenly I noticed that I felt lighter, with an air of joy welling up inside me. It was as though eight hundred pounds of weight had instantly lifted from me. Joy sprang up from somewhere inside like a newfound revelation, and I thought, *Wow, what is this? I feel like I am somehow different!*

I thought about telling my roommate what had just occurred but quickly decided that my words were probably cheap at that point. I would let him see the changes that had taken place as I walked out this new faith day by day. That is what I made up my mind to do. I knew I had to do something with this joy I was experiencing, so I threw on my running shoes and commenced to run my three-mile training route at a blistering pace, fueled by this joy-adrenaline that was surging through me.

When I finished the run I was truly tired. I wondered what this new life, this new journey, held for me. Whatever it was to be, I knew that this would be the start of walking with Jesus as a disciple.

To Be a Disciple

To be a disciple is to say *yes* to Jesus Christ. This is an all-in decision to risk everything and trust that God is ultimately and unwaveringly good, as he shows us through the gift of his Son on that lonely cross. That offering stands for all eternity as conclusive evidence that, right now, at this moment, God's love is still the greatest truth in our lives. No matter what, he sent Jesus. No matter what, Jesus Christ rose from the dead. No matter what, this is a living, moving, daily reality that cannot be minimized and, in fact, is able to grow within us in myriad ways that can continually cause wonder and excitement about the possibilities of what God will do!

The Path of Discipleship

The *path* of discipleship. I am giving the term "path" a broad definition here that is open-ended and looks as varied as the faces of those who follow

Jesus worldwide. He created us individually, loves us individually, and walks with us individually. My walk as a disciple will be different from yours. Are there some commonalities or some similarities? Of course. We see this in the way Jesus taught many things that apply to all his disciples. Yet he spoke to each individually about his particular call to them and what he was asking each to do and participate in.

He knows us, he understands the potential inside of us, and he has gifted us all individually. Yes, there is also a corporate purpose in the body of Christ, but to me the beauty, the strength, and the passion are in that individual relationship with the Lord in which he strengthens, comforts, encourages, and challenges each one of us to be the one *he* knows we can be—the name he calls us and the destiny toward which he propels us. When we are equipped to be part of the worldwide body of Christ, we are gifted to participate in discipleship as we collectively seek the lost and pursue Jesus's invitation to make disciples of every nation.

To Be a Disciple Will Cost Something

"When Jesus calls a man, He bids him come and die." This declaration, written by Dietrich Bonhoeffer, the WWII Christian pastor, theologian, and martyr, is the staunch reality we need to understand when we place our trust in Jesus Christ. Many people place their trust in Christ's sacrificial death for salvation, a step often referred to as conversion, but my contention is that, without a life of discipleship that costs everything, there has probably been no true conversion.

Let that sink in. The one who thinks, *Well, I have put my hope in Christ, and therefore I believe and am saved,* yet has no inward and outward dedication to the call of Jesus Christ is in grave danger of believing wrongly about what salvation in Christ truly is. Salvation—true salvation—saves us from something: eternal judgment. More importantly, it saves us *to* something: a life of obedience to the call of Jesus Christ to follow to the point of death—and, along the way, the challenge and adventure of being a disciple who makes disciples.

This might be a good time to take a moment, put this book down, and consider what your belief has done in you. Are you truly following Jesus Christ, obeying his great call, and putting aside distractions and wrongful pastimes in order to seek him? Do you endeavor to hear his teachings through his Word? Or are you walking in a life that *you* have designed, side-stepping the hard reality of standing for Christ without considering what pleases him? Are you ready to turn to him completely and ask for his heart for people?

Again, take some time and consider . . . Your first call is to Jesus Christ himself. He holds the future for you to participate in and offers it as an invitation. His invitation is for you to take part in a grand story that is more epic than you could ever imagine.

I have always been enamored with stories that show the excitement, intrigue, fear, and wonder of a journey. C. S. Lewis's *The Lion, The Witch, and the Wardrobe* is the beginning of one such series. Another is J. R. R. Tolkien's The Lord of the Rings trilogy. Both of these authors creatively tell stories that are analogous to the Christian life. In both cases there are naïveté and innocence, interrupted by an invitation to something mysterious and wonderful . . . a new journey! And the journey always takes the characters into something much greater than themselves. Yet, because youthfulness and innocence do not have a well-developed sense of caution and adequate wisdom, each journey becomes perilous and stunning to the point of discouragement and death, with characters giving up hope until another hero arrives. And he does!

This is a simplistic way to identify such classic stories, but they are accurate in describing the true Christian experience: there is excitement at new birth; intrigue that illuminates the path as we learn that God is leading to places we have not adventured in before; fear when we learn the reality that we have been invited into to a war, not a picnic; and wonder as we participate in things seen and unseen that only a holy, creative, loving God would dare to craft for us, so much larger than our own lives, yet needing our participation to fulfill a grand plan.

Discipleship has a beginning, but it has no end, unless, of course, you factor in that we will one day be called from this earth to participate in another world, at a new level, in the heavenly kingdom that awaits us as we hope in Christ. Wow. This journey, your story, my story, our story, has a really good ending! Along the way, however, excitement, intrigue, fear, and wonder await us. Are you all in?

Chapter 3

The Call of a Disciple and the Word of God

There is no endeavor and no higher call, personal or corporate, than the invitation into the Word of God. The Word of God, the holy Scripture, is more than simply text on pages. The Word of God is what it proclaims itself to be: the very thoughts and breath of the living God. Yes, the words on the pages are ancient, yet they are alive! I love this truth from Hebrews 4:12 in the Amplified Bible: "For the word of God is living and active *and* full of power [making it operative, energizing, and effective]. It is sharper than any two-edged sword, penetrating as far as the division of the soul and spirit [the completeness of a person], and of both joints and marrow [the deepest parts of our nature], exposing *and* judging the very thoughts and intentions of the heart."

The word is alive! Hebrews 4:12 describes the Word of God as a scalpel in the hands of a surgeon. Piercing, judging, separating. This is the activity of a skilled heavenly physician, using his Spirit-empowered words to permeate deeper into us than anything else we have ever experienced. And he does this out of love, to see us become who he has created us to be. He guides this process carefully.

When we open the Word of God, we can do so with one of many attitudes. We can believe we are entering into a dry academic process of study (sounds like drudgery, as in the most boring high school or college class), or we can enter into the Word of God as though we have been given an invitation to a banquet with a king.

Mary showcases this so well in Luke 10:38–42. You probably know the story. As Jesus visited the home of Mary and Martha, two sisters who were his disciples, Martha was running around trying to make preparations for him and his entourage of disciples. Mary, however, sat on the floor at Jesus's feet listening to the words he spoke. When Martha complained to Jesus that Mary needed to help with the preparations, Jesus responded that Martha was worried about things that were quite insignificant, while Mary had chosen what was better, . . . and it wouldn't be taken from her.

The gentle conviction that comes from this scene reminds me to enter into my time with Jesus, as Mary did, gazing upon the Word of God; this posture is like gazing into the eyes of Jesus Himself, taking in every word he has to say. I'll have to admit that there were many times in my earlier years when I treated the Word of God and the study of the Word as something I needed to check off on the list of what I was doing as a follower of Christ. This activity was no more than an item on a to-do list, without consideration of what his words possibly held for me.

I unintentionally adopted the attitude that, if I simply read the Word in the morning in a cursory fashion—my religious duty—I would be good to go for the day. The problem with that type of thinking is that it misses the point that Jesus was emphasizing to Martha: to be with Jesus is to set everything else aside and let him speak. Our time with the Word of God should be just that: an opportunity to ask the Spirit to speak to us as we open the pages of Scripture.

This is intended to be a delight, and it becomes so when we begin with the understanding that God, as a loving Father, wants to spend time with you and me! Spending time with him is truly what he created us for. James, the author of the New Testament letter of James and a leader of the early church, was Jesus's brother and had grown up alongside him. James, probably more than anyone else, knew his brother's heart for relationships. James declares in James 4 that God jealously longs for connection with the spirit he has placed in us. Could there a greater manifestation of God's desire to meet with us? He jealously longs to commune with our spirit. That is how he abides with us, speaks with us, and shares himself with us . . . and we are to offer the same in return.

A further note: What will heaven be like? Won't we long to be near the Father and the Son? When we see them, won't we run, crashing into their arms in desperate longing for the love we were created to experience together with them? And won't we delight to hold and draw close to every loved one who has gone before us, not to mention the ancient brothers and sisters in the faith we have read about so often, wondering what they are truly like? Personally, I look forward to the time when all of these things will take place!

The Word *is* Jesus . . . In John 1 the author writes, "In the beginning was the Word, and the Word was with God, and the Word was God." Obviously the

Word is synonymous with Jesus. In verse 14 John writes, "The Word became flesh and made his dwelling among us. We have seen his glory, the glory of the one and only Son, who came from the Father, full of grace and truth." It is interesting to note that, when God the Father wanted to reveal himself to us, he did so by sending his Word: Jesus. Jesus, the Son, is the revealed Word of God. If you want to know what God is like, look at Jesus. We can "read" Jesus's life like a book sent from the Father to show his will and his heart toward us.

In Genesis 1 Moses wrote that God created *through his words* (in verse 1 the Hebrew word for God is *Elohim*, which is plural—meaning that Jesus and the Holy Spirit are present with—indeed, are *one* with—the Father). God spoke those words through Jesus, who *is* the Word, as stated in John 1. When God gave the revelation of himself to people, he spoke, and we read his spoken words in the Bible.

The Bible was written over the course of 1500 years by prophets, teachers, shepherds, statesmen, historians, poets, and others. The Bible has 66 books and 783,137 words (KJV) and is the best-selling book of all time. The Bible was not written at the behest of those who penned its pages but by the will and direction of almighty God, and it declares of itself that his breath inspired those who wrote and that the same Spirit of God is able to reveal truth and apply it to each one of us as we read the words of Scripture today.

Here's the best part: we have an invitation from the author himself to sit with him and seek him through his Word to know his will and to experience his great love being revealed and renewed in and for us every day.

Get Up and Get into the Word

One of the keys to a relationship with the Father that is fresh and new every day is establishing a time and place to spend time with Jesus in the morning. I am not thinking "religiously" at all as I share this with you but am coming from a sense of freedom. The most important part of my day is with Jesus as I seek him early, every new morning. This is the delight of my heart because I know it is also the delight of his heart!

As I sit down in the morning to open the Word of God, I ask the Holy Spirit to open my eyes and ears and to show me what he wants me to see in his Word. The Jewish rabbis had a statement, "The Torah has 70 faces." If the Jewish teachers believed that there are seventy faces in the Old Testament law, just what is made available to us in the Word that fulfills and transcends the law? How exciting it is to know that the Lord wants to reveal his Word in a myriad of fresh ways every morning! We have the invitation to learn, seek, read, ask, search, listen, and receive through the Word of God.

It may be that you lack confidence that you will understand the Bible. Allow me to help you with that. A small beginning is all you need. Take, for example, starting with the New Testament book of Matthew. It is one of the four Gospels that describe the life of Jesus. Each Gospel (meaning "Good News") is written from a different lens, as seen by another of the disciples with a perspective similar to and yet different from that of the others who wrote. This allows for greater clarity about the life of Jesus.

My suggestion is to start with Matthew and read one or two chapters each morning. As you do, take time to consider questions like: Who is this chapter about? What is the main idea or issue in this section? Is there a verse that stands out to me as I read this section? How can I apply what I read to my life? Noticing something that stands out to you as you read Scripture and then taking the time to think about its connection to something—even yourself—is a powerful way to read and learn about the Bible. For example, when you read in Matthew 5:14, "You are the light of the world. A town built on a hill cannot be hidden," apply the questions I suggested.

Who is this about, or, in this case, who is talking? This is Jesus declaring to his disciples You count. You share the light of Jesus. This is a reminder to you of that truth.

What is the main idea? The main idea is that Jesus is telling the disciples— who include you and me—that what he came to be and to give, the light of heaven, is who we are and what we can give to people.

Is there a verse, a clause, or a phrase that stands out? To me, it's, "You are the light of the world." How impactful! How inspiring!

How can I apply this verse to my life? I can consider the truth Jesus is speaking and make the decision to represent him as his light to those around me.

Another great help in reading and studying the Bible is keeping a journal. Journaling can be done in hard copy with pen and paper or online with your own format—a document or note page. Create your own pages. You can be as academic as you like, or you can approach this creatively, perhaps with pictures and story maps, bullet points, and diagrams. The options are wide open to your imagination.

Why journal? When you write about the Scripture truths you read, you double your comprehension and recall. Also, you begin to take the Word of God more deeply into your mind, your soul, and your spirit. The Word of God has his mind and breath in it, so it begins to fill you as you spend more time with it by writing what you are thinking about the ideas and truths you have just read.

Some of the highest levels of thinking are analysis and evaluation. As you record your observations, you are expanding your thoughts and assimilating the text into a new level of understanding. This provides for what the Bible calls in Romans 12:2 a "renewed" mind. Science shows that the brain is always capable of creating new pathways.[1] Even your old habits of thought and belief are subject to change as you take in God's Word, write about it, and act on it!

It is highly important to note that God is never disappointed in the time you spend or the amount you take in from him. That is up to you to decide. The Lord simply loves to be with you. As an example, when my kids, who are now grown, ask me if I would like to join them for coffee or a bite to eat or help with a project, my response is an invariable and absolute yes. I enjoy the time we have together, whether short or long. I realize they want to spend time with me, which blesses my heart, and I am thankful for our relationship.

Time is not a factor. I was privileged to help bring them into the world, and my goal as they grew up was to see them develop mature, healthy relationships that they would invest in. I am incredibly fortunate to enjoy these mature friendships with my kids. I do not have expectations of them that are negative or demanding . . . they get to experience freedom with me, freedom based on the way I have learned that God, as my heavenly Father, treats me. He loves our relationship and enjoys every minute of it. So do I!

I understand that God knows I am finite in the scope of my thinking. I wish I could spend more time with my thoughts devoted to him and more time in prayer with him. I continually grow in these regards, yet I realize that I am human and limited. I am very thankful that God as my heavenly Father knows and loves me as I am, enjoying me as he created me . . . imperfect, yet beautiful to him in friendship and partnership.

Devotional within Your Wheelhouse

There are two basic types of personality groups we all are accustomed to, with a variety of nuances. The first we call the Type A and the second the Type B personality group.[2] Type A personalities are known for being goal-oriented and precise, which can sometimes be an issue when it comes to a devotional time in the morning in that this tendency can lend itself to the feeling of having to keep a routine or schedule that becomes either monotonous or, on the other hand, can never be infringed upon by other elements. Individuals with Type A personalities will want to keep in mind that God is a lover of our time with him, not a judge or heavy-handed taskmaster.

Likewise, those with Type B personalities, who are typically laid-back and easy-going, will want to understand that a routine in and of itself is not a religious obligation and does not need to be lacking in freedom and creativity. In fact, it is a great idea to establish a routine that keeps us guided by the Father and yet open to creative endeavors and changes that allow for fresh winds and ideas. Relax! Take your time with the Lord according to the way you are wired and look forward to the growth he will bring.

Chapter 4

To Be a Disciple:
How to Engage in the Word of God and Receive from the Lord Every Day

When you begin the day with any devotional, what you will begin to notice is that your thinking changes over time. Rather than engaging in your run-of-the-mill thinking, your mind gets set on higher things. From seemingly out of nowhere, you will have thoughts about the Lord, about heaven, and about what he may be doing in your life or a nudge to pray for someone. You see, when you begin to take in the Word of God, you automatically get an infusion of his Spirit and his presence, which carries with it his influence.

The Word of God is alive and dynamic, after all! If the Word is active in you, then it moves in your system: your mind, your soul, and your spirit. By the way, the Word of God begins to dislodge and displace older, weaker forms of thinking and even habits. Please understand that we are talking about the most powerful influence in the universe—the most powerful influence ever known in human history, the very words of its Creator God.

A side note: The devil, the enemy of our souls, is hell bent on minimizing the power of the Word of God to and in us. He will denounce it, instigate doubt, and use circumstances to cause us to question the validity and power of the Word. Yet notice that, as Jesus was in the wilderness with Satan being tempted and tested, his first and continued response was to refute Satan *with* the Word of God.

Jesus was quick thinking, authoritative, and steadfast, and he is the example for us to follow. We need to realize that Jesus was setting the standard we are to use. He demonstrated how victory is won over the devil and his forces, assuring us that we also will win by reverting back to the Word of God. That Word is, after all, our shield and sword. I can't emphasize enough the importance of reading and becoming more familiar with the brilliance and wisdom of God's Word every day.

As we read, we prepare ourselves for so much more than we currently understand. There are situations and circumstances ahead of us that we are being prepared for by the Word of God as we absorb it day after day. There is an old adage that states, "Luck is what happens when preparation meets opportunity." While I don't believe in luck, personally, I believe in the concept here - preparation for anything and everything up ahead is the overriding idea. The smart athlete trains for the competition ahead; the smart financier saves for the ups and downs of economics in the future; the wise student prepares day after day for the exams that await; and the devoted Christian, the disciple who is following the teachings of our Lord and Savior Jesus Christ, reads, prays, and believes in the Word of God and so is being readied for the trials and opportunities ahead.

As you endeavor to live your life as a disciple, the Word of God and your steadfast devotion to it will be a gauge and determiner of your successful living for the Lord. As you spend more time in the Scriptures, especially the Gospels, you will understand more and more the teachings and thinking of Jesus.

This is the way you learn his voice. Jesus declared in John 10:27, "My sheep listen to my voice; I know them, and they follow me." The Holy Spirit of God will bring the words of Jesus to mind. He will elaborate on them in your thinking so that your mentality is stirred by his Word in you. The Spirit of God wants you to recognize and respond to his voice and promptings, which will become familiar from the Scriptures you read.

To Be a Disciple, Learn How the Bible Is Organized

Most people know that the Bible is arranged into two distinct yet related parts, the Old Testament and the New Testament. What is the difference?

A short and simple explanation is what you need to begin with.

The Old Testament is the part of the Bible that describes God's work in creation, his call to the ancient saints to follow him, the inception of the nation of Israel, the subsequent history of the activities of this chosen nation, books of wisdom and poetry, and prophetic writings that describe the Messiah who would come, as well as some future events.

The Old Testament holds the stories of the saints who went before us; their lives are laid out before us so that we can learn of their mistakes, as well as their victories. We can be encouraged by the stories of those who went before us because each one was human, as we are, and like us prone to weakness. God worked in them and through them in spite of their limitations and personal issues. The apostle Paul wrote to the Corinthian church, "Now these things happened to them as an example, and they were written for our instruction, upon whom the ends of the ages have come" (1 Corinthians 10:11 NASB).

The same apostle penned similar wisdom to the Roman church: "For everything that was written in the past was written to teach us, so that through the endurance taught in the Scriptures and the encouragement they provide we might have hope" (Romans 15:4). Still today we can learn and become wise through the Old Testament's authors.

Break It Down

This will be a brief breakdown of what the Old Testament contains. For a more exhaustive study, there are many great books and commentaries to give you a deeper experience of both the Old and New Testaments. For our purposes, I will simply give a general overview here.

Genesis is the grand story of creation. Genesis describes the rise and fall of the first family and especially the gracious intervention and rescue by the Lord God, displaying his love and mercy. The first five books of the Old Testament, written by Moses, are called the Torah, the Hebrew word meaning teaching, direction, guidance, or law. The next books, Joshua through Esther, chronicle Israel's history.

Job through Song of Songs (known from some translations as the Song of Solomon) are known as the poetic books. They are filled with creative beauty of language, along with great thoughts and statements of wisdom we can apply to our lives. The prophetic books follow with what are known as the major prophets, Isaiah through Daniel. These prophetic books are filled with prophecies of the coming Messiah, along with future events concerning Israel and the nations of the world. The minor prophets complete the Old Testament and include Hosea through Malachi.

The Old Testament consists of 39 books. The overarching divine authorship is a continuing theme throughout, even though the actual books were written over the span of about 1000 years by at least twenty-four different known human authors, from kings and shepherds to prophets, statesmen, and observers of God's works. The Old Testament displays the lives of many who were true to God's call and showcases the ways they stood for the Lord and how God used them to change families, nations, and the known world.

However, the Old Testament is also very clear about what happens when people do not trust God or cease to believe and fall away. The Old Testament is honest in every historical scenario so that we can be encouraged in our own walk of faith with the Lord.

The New Testament consists of 27 books, with at least nine different authors. The first four are historical books that are called the Gospels, meaning Good News. They reveal the good news of God's Messiah, Jesus Christ, coming to the earth and describe the way he lived, taught, related to all types of people, died, rose from the dead, and instituted his church on the earth.

After the four opening Gospels of Matthew, Mark, Luke, and John comes the last historical book, the Acts of the Apostles. This is the record of Jesus leaving the Earth to return to heaven and sending his Holy Spirit into the world to birth and guide the new church that would represent him and through which he would continue his work. In the book of Acts, a major player emerges named Saul, who was, incredibly, on a mission to destroy the early church by arresting the disciples of Jesus and having them either thrown into prison or put to death.

As Saul was on his mission, he was confronted by the risen and ascended Jesus, who appeared dramatically to him. Saul was transformed by Jesus Christ and became one of the most significant persons in the New Testament record. Saul, whose name was changed to Paul, went on to write thirteen of the New Testament books, including the next books of the Bible after Acts, which record his instructions as to how a follower of Christ should live and how churches should operate under the guidance of the Holy Spirit with biblical leadership.

After Paul's writings appear a series of letters written by other followers of Jesus Christ, such as Peter, James, Jude, and John. The New Testament ends with what we know as the Revelation. This is the testimony of Jesus Christ, revealing to his servant John the Apostle instructions for the churches that were in existence at that time. The book of Revelation includes prophetic teachings about world history that would unfold and grandiose apocalyptic scenarios, depicting how the end of the world will take place, leading to Jesus setting up his eternal kingdom.

Getting Started

A great idea when starting to study the Bible is to find a Bible that includes what is called commentary, often in the form of study notes. There are many great Bible scholars who have written their comments at the bottom of the pages of Scripture so that you can get an enhanced understanding of the meaning. In addition, many separate commentaries are available in book form or on the Internet. No one commentator knows everything, and there are differing interpretations and emphases, so it is always good to consult a variety of sources when trying to understand the Bible and its doctrines—those foundational truths that come from Scripture that believers rely on for life and faith.

While some doctrines are relatively easily understood—such as the historical truths of the life, death, and resurrection of Jesus Christ—others can be challenging and are debated as to the correct or complete meaning. Where this is true, commentaries can help provide a fresh perspective and meaning.

An important understanding you will need as a disciple is the reality that you will continually grow in your understanding of the Word of God as the Holy Spirit makes you steadily more aware of its implications and nuances. Your views may evolve as you grow, and this is good and expected. Some Scriptures are hard to understand early on but take on ever richer meaning with continued study, as well as with learning more about history and context. As with any other endeavor, the more time and effort you put in, the more you will get out of the Word!

The Principle of Starting Fresh

The beginning of the day. Fresh, replete with possibility, and wide open. Imagine being one of the early disciples following Jesus around the shores of the Sea of Galilee. You awake to each new morning with the first person you see being Jesus the Messiah. You begin the day hearing his voice, his words, and following Jesus along the seashore, through villages, and along desert roads.

You have a deep feeling of excitement because you know there is a fresh purpose and a renewed sense that this journey is larger than yourself, and you know you have been invited to take part in a grand story. Where are you going today? What is the next teaching that will cause wonder and amazement? What will Jesus do for people today (you recall hearing hundreds of requests to see the Messiah, to hear him, and to be touched by him), and what will your part be?

And so, you set out, filled with awe and wonder.

I believe Jesus's intention and invitation remain the same for every disciple who follows him still. He is waiting every new morning as we rise, waiting to meet us with a gleam in his eye. He looks at us with confidence, knowing we are following him and trust him. He is excited about the day and begins to move in a particular direction, beckoning us to follow. He begins to reveal words of truth as he speaks to us.

At first we're not sure what it all means, but as we listen it becomes clearer. He tells us about the Father, about reaching the lost, about caring for the needs of those around us, and especially about the Father's great love and mercy for us and for the world. Suddenly the message he is instilling settles deeper within, and we experience a sense of awe as we begin to understand the depth of the Father's heart for the world and are changed a bit more and ready to do the Father's will.

"He wakens me morning by morning, wakens my ear to listen as one being instructed. (Isaiah 50:4)

"Very early in the morning, while it was still dark, Jesus got up, left the house and went out to a solitary place, where he prayed." (Mark 1:35)

"But seek first his kingdom and his righteousness, and all these things will be given to you as well." (Matthew 6:33)

There is a principle here that the Lord sets forth, the principle of starting each new day in his presence, hearing (reading) his words, considering what he is teaching us, and then having a conversation with the Lord through prayer.

I do realize that there are many who have more of a challenge with the shifts they work, children who have challenging sleep schedules, and a host of other issues. Please consider how the idea of a fresh time to meet with the Lord may apply to your circumstances.

The commitment to daily devotional time with the Lord is the X-factor in the life of a disciple. There are many people with whom I have been in a discipleship relationship or who are considering becoming serious about the Lord who have balked at this principle. The usual line of reasoning is something like, "I get up really early already" or, "I pray many times during the day" or, "I fit in my devotions at lunch, or at bedtime at night—this relaxes me." There are plenty of other reasons people offer for not starting fresh with the Lord at the onset of each new day in a devotional relationship.

Let me be clear, I am not trying to set up a behavioral religious process or look at someone's lifestyle and schedule and judge it for "righteousness" based on my ideals. This is really about the heart and about setting yourself up to know the Lord better by giving the first, and often the most alert, part of your day to him in fellowship.

Maybe an example will help.

As a married man, I can't imagine hopping out of bed in the morning, day after day, without speaking to my wife or spending time listening to her or sharing some time in communication. That would not be relational at all and certainly wouldn't show that we love each other. Likewise, I can't imagine trying to be a good father who cares about his kids but doesn't speak a word to them in the morning, instead getting my "business as usual" taken care of with only a casual glance at them and without communicating my love and affection.

In contrast, what a blessing for my wife when I build in time in the morning to spend in conversation with her, to pray together, and to talk about the day and all that is on our minds! What a blessing for every kid growing up when a mom or dad takes the time to sit for a few minutes and discuss the coming day with them—to provide relationship, security, and perspective, and most of all to be available and receptive.

For those of you who cite reasons that the morning is not the best occasion for devotional time with the Lord, I would ask you to at least consider this verse and its application.

"Taste and see that the LORD is good; blessed is the one who takes refuge in him." (Psalm 34:8)

When do you first eat every day? For many, if not most of us, isn't it in the morning? And why is that? To get nourishment, to be sustained. See the connection? When is the best time for the nourishment and sustaining of our soul? Again, right away in the morning.

Let me explain this through a short teaching.

We are each comprised of three parts, as most would recognize: body, soul, and spirit. The body is obviously all things physical, along with our five senses. The soul can be expressed as the mind, agency or will, and emotions. The spirit is the inner person, the eternal breath of life that God speaks to and inhabits in the disciple.

Our body needs food and water in order to be nourished and sustained properly. We are usually in tune with our physical needs and take care of them regularly. When we get hungry, or worse, do not eat for a long period of time, the results are tangible: fatigue, exhaustion, and even sickness. Our souls need nourishment as well; this comes in the form of love, respect, care, and positive relationships, as well as the opportunity to use our minds purposefully. Similarly, when the soul is not nourished correctly, life deteriorates and is neither positive nor pleasant. Proper soul nourishment is vital. Positive inputs, relationships, and purpose fill us and keep us mentally and emotionally healthy.

It is the same for the spirit, that unseen area in which the Lord resides. Our spirit is the centerpiece of our existence in Christ. The spirit is nourished by the Word of God, prayer, worship, fellowship, and service for God's purposes. We probably do not realize that our spirit is as sensitive as our physical selves and as intuitive as our soul. When the spirit is not nourished, we become spiritually exhausted, experience little or no joy or purpose, and can become self-centered and lonely.

People are healthiest when they take care of their bodies and souls at the start of the day. This is common sense, is it not? Likewise, your spirit craves the Word and presence of God each new day. This is the bread from heaven. Like new blooms in the early spring, growing in the warmth of the sunshine and enriched by the fresh spring rains, we are enriched by God's presence within us, filling us early, nurturing us, and touching everything in us with his powerful words of refreshment and healing.

So, let me ask you, What is your current morning routine? Is your pattern of living allowing the Lord to move in you in fresh new ways every morning? Remember, you were created for a relationship with the Father, and he longs to have fellowship with you, a friendship that allows him to show you ever greater levels of his love, mercy, grace, power, and purpose. Once you fall into the pattern of this kind of fellowship, you will continually grow and weather every type of season, enduring and being receptive to the Lord's goodness, sustaining power, presence, and purpose.

Being a Disciple Who Takes the Word of God Deeper

Memorize the Word of God.

When I first became a follower of Christ, I knew nothing about the Christian life, the Bible, and Christian thinking. I had a good friend who led me and truly was a mentor, helping me understand how to read the Word of God. His name is Jeff Williams. I mentioned him earlier as having shared Bible verses with me when we were in high school, but he was also the one who wanted to share the discipleship process with me early on, when I was a new follower in Jesus.

Jeff spent a great deal of time teaching me to understand how to read the Word of God in context, and one of the things we did regularly was to take a Scripture verse or passage and memorize it. This was fun to do as friends, and I remember going over several Bible verses then that are still to this day held as core values in my heart and mind. I didn't realize it then, but memorizing Scripture was setting me up to retain the Word of God, which the Lord would bring to my mind at key times to help form in my mind God-centered thinking.

For me as a disciple, I can think of several reasons to commit the Word of God to memory. First, this is the way you internalize the Scriptures so that they blend into your thinking. David, the psalmist and king, wrote in Psalm 1, "Blessed is the one who does not walk in step with the wicked or stand in the way that sinners take or sit in the seat of mockers, but whose delight is in the law of the LORD, and who meditates on his law day and night. That person is like a tree planted by streams of water, which yields its fruit in season and whose leaf does not wither—whatever they do prospers." He also wrote in Psalm 119:11, "I have hidden your word in my heart that I might not sin against you."

One of the ways to hide God's Word inside your heart is to memorize it. A simple way to get started is to write down a verse on a 3 x 5 card or type it on a phone app and place it where you will see it often. Put it in your pocket or purse and take it out several times a day to look at it and read it. If you speak it out loud, your comprehension doubles. I like to split a verse into parts, taking one part at a time and reciting it over and over until I feel I have it somewhat memorized. Then I will do the same with the next part. Finally, I will try it all together. This process transfers the verse from my short-term to my long-term memory, and that takes repetition.

There is a well-known picture of what meditating on the Word of God looks like. This picture, counterintuitive as it may seem, is of a cow chewing its cud. Let me explain. When I was growing up, I spent time on my grand-parents' farm in New Brunswick, Canada. My grandfather had milking cows that he tended to every day. On some occasions he would let me tag along as he herded them into the barn and into their stanchions to be milked, and on rare occasions he would take me with him if a cow had somehow gotten out of the fenced area around the farm.

Cows can be interesting to watch. When they were in the fields grazing, I noticed that they would eat grass and chew it slowly. Sometimes it seemed as though the process were never ending. Because grass is hard to digest, the cow would chew it for a while, swallow it, and then regurgitate it back up, only to chew and then swallow it again. This process allowed the cow to better process and digest the grass—the food.

Meditating on the Word of God, the Scriptures, can be understood similarly. As we read a passage, we take time to think about its meaning and how it applies to us or others. This is how we "chew" on the Word of God. When we go back to that verse or passage again and again, like the cow with her cud, we are further processing the meaning and application, digesting it more completely until it is fully processed. The Word of God is called bread by Jesus. It's food. Much as the cow's cud eventually becomes nourishing food, the Word of God that is meditated upon becomes food for us and those around us. Peter the apostle enjoined his readers, "Crave pure spiritual milk, so that by it you may grow up in your salvation" (1 Peter 2:2).

Circling back to the teaching about body, soul, and spirit, when you meditate on the Word of God and learn it by memorizing the text, you take the Word beyond the mind and soul into the spirit, that deep place inside you that God entered and brought to life within you. Your spirit longs to be filled with this type of spiritual food. When your spirit receives the Word of God, it moves within you to build faith and strengthen your inner self.

Resolve wells up from the Word of God hidden deep within you. God uses that Word to awaken you to more truth and to maturity in him. The more time you spend with the Scriptures, the more you feed the hunger in your spirit for communion with God; the more you prepare yourself for the tests and trials ahead; and the more you find delight in the Lord, which gives you peace mentally, physically, emotionally, and spiritually. "My son, pay attention to what I say; turn your ear to my words. Do not let them out of your sight, keep them within your heart; for they are life to those who find them and health to one's whole body" (Proverbs 4:20–22). God wants us to receive and walk in health that permeates our whole system, gleaned by listening to and obeying his Word.

How does the Word of God fill your spirit and build you up? By way of explanation, I'll refer to a biblical event. In Exodus 16 in the Old Testament, the Israelites were grumbling about not having food. God provided what Moses called "bread from the Lord." Understand that, according to biblical scholars, there were probably over two million people in the desert at this time.[3] But every night God sent down fresh bread, "manna," as it was called.

The Israelites were instructed to gather just enough each morning for the day. Interesting, they were to gather the bread from heaven each new morning, not relying on yesterday's food from heaven but accepting it fresh and new every morning. Sounds rather like Jeremiah's words in Lamentations 3:23: "His mercies are new every morning." Or like Jesus's declaration in John 6:58, "I am the true bread that came down out of heaven." When we take in the Word of God, we are taking in the bread of heaven: Jesus.

He is the Word, just as he is the bread. His presence is in every word because he is the Word of God. He is alive, and therefore his Word is living. This brings up Hebrews 4:12 once again: "For the word of God is alive and active. Sharper than any double-edged sword, it penetrates even to dividing soul and spirit, joints and marrow; it judges the thoughts and attitudes of the heart." Because Jesus is the life and breath of the Word, because he *is* the Word, when you take in the Word of God you take in Jesus, more and more. More of the Word, more Jesus. He fills, enables, comforts, encourages, listens, prepares, heals, empowers, sends, and builds you up!

How closely do you want to experience Jesus? How closely do you think he wants to experience you?

Jesus created you to know him—intimately so. He wants you to experience who he is and how powerfully he loves you. He created you physically, as a place, a residence, within which he can live. He likes to dwell with you and in you, and he always wants to be where you are. He made sure that would happen when you invited him to change your life.

According to the words of Jesus, when you repented of your sins and placed your faith in his death on the cross for your forgiveness, trusting in his resurrection from the dead as your power for living, the Spirit of God took up residence inside you, "cleaning house," so to speak. He washed away your sin and gave you a heart that is sensitive to him, a mind that can understand the Word of God, and a spirit that is alive in him! He occupied your entire system, changing your heart spiritually and promising to never reject you or leave you. You are never alone.

If you are a guy—he calls you a son. If you are a girl—he calls you a daughter. He claims you as his own and wants to continually speak to you. His words, his voice, flow from the Word of God you take in. You will experience the very real and personal love of God through his presence that illuminates his Word to your spirit, soul, and body.

Chapter 5

Being a Disciple Who Prays

I love prayer. But let's be honest. Prayer can be hard at times. Still, I love the invitation to speak with the author and Creator of the universe. I've never had a king or president reach out to me for conversation—but daily I have the greatest king, the greatest leader, the most intelligent author and Creator of all things, both seen and unseen, reach out and want to discuss with me my life, my family, my career, and the people around me and his love for them. This is an incredible truth that is beyond my capability to understand.

In our day and age, it seems as though everyone is busy . . . sometimes too busy. Many people I spend time with want to talk about their lives, their hopes, their fears, and their future. And I love to listen. It is an honor to be trusted with such important revelations from someone's life. There are times when I, too, need someone to listen when I want to express myself . . . and God as a Father opens up his ears every day and invites me to unpack with him everything that is on my mind and in my heart. He loves to hear and respond to it all.

Have you ever spent time with a three-year-old and listened to the little one prattle on and on about what they were playing, complete with all the details and ideas bubbling forth from their young, creative imagination? Or how about a high school senior explaining their anticipated next steps, next chapters, hopes, concerns, dreams, and plans? Have you ever sat with an aging parent or friend in their last few years—or months—as they reflected on their life, allowing you to listen in on the memories that tumbled out, to their historical memoir spilling out as you listened?

The Lord of the universe, Creator and sustainer of all things, longs to hear from you the same way you patiently listen to a three-year-old, a high school senior, or an aging friend or loved one. He delights in us! The one who "sings over us" (Zephaniah 3:17) and has "engraved [your name] on the palms of my hands" (Isaiah 49:16) experiences ceaseless joy over you. Our Father loves to walk with you and listen. Yet he also longs to reveal himself to you. Jesus shows this to us in John 14:21, "Whoever has my commands and keeps them is the one who loves me. The one who loves me will be loved by my Father, and I too will love them and show myself to them." The time we spend with the Lord is precious to him. He wants to reveal himself in increasingly meaningful ways, ways he opens up through his Word and prayer.

God invites you into conversation with him! God loves partnership and created us with this in mind, that we would be partners together with him in his work. But how can we understand the partnership if we don't ask the Father *how* he wants us to partner with him? Jesus said more than once, "Whoever has ears, let them hear." (Matthew 11:15), and he also stated of himself, "... the Son can do nothing by himself; he can do only what he sees his father doing..." (John 5:19).

Jesus knew how to partner with his Father: he asked. One of the most frequently used words for prayer in the New Testament is the Greek *aiteo*, which carries the translation "ask." It is used in this way over sixty times in the New Testament. Jesus asked his Father many things; this is something he had to have done over and over again every day, for, as he also said, "I . . . do exactly what my Father has commanded me" (John 14:31).

What a great model for us to follow! We can ask the Father anything, and he hears us, longing to give us the answer. Have you ever stopped and asked God, "Father, what would please you in terms of this decision?" It is imperative that we, as disciples of Jesus, follow the example of Jesus and learn to ask the Father about the things we are trying to decide.

Let me hasten to point out, however, that we can easily take this a bit too far down the road? For example, if I have a choice for breakfast between oatmeal and eggs, do I need to ask the Father about that one? Probably not. When I'm shopping and have to decide among brands of a certain item, do I pray about that? Again, probably not. However, there are decisions we make every day that include one or more choices that have important direction attached to them. Those decisions could be prayed about. The more often we get into the habit of asking the Lord about our direction, the more we will know which choices to ask about. Bottom line: when in doubt, ask!

There is a scenario from the Old Testament book of Joshua that informs us about how necessary it is to ask the Father about our plans. When Joshua took the leadership of Israel after Moses's death, he immediately sought the

Lord about how to take the land God had promised to the Israelites through Abraham. When Joshua asked, the Lord answered, and when the Lord answered Joshua acted on those words with obedience and Israel prevailed. At one point in the taking of the land, Israel was routing every nation around them, and some of the nearby nations became afraid of Israel and their God. Gibeon, a nation nearby, decided to pull a fast one on Joshua and the Israelites. Here is a synopsis of the story from Joshua 9:

When the people of Gibeon heard what Joshua had done to Jericho and Ai, they resorted to a ruse: they went as a delegation whose donkeys were loaded with worn-out sacks and old wineskins, cracked and mended. They put worn and patched sandals on their feet and wore old clothes. All the bread in their food supply was dry and moldy. Then they went to Joshua in the camp at Gilgal and said to him and the Israelites, "We have come from a distant country; make a treaty with us . . ."

The Israelites sampled their provisions *but did not inquire of the Lord.* Then Joshua made a treaty of peace with them to let them live, and the leaders of the assembly ratified it by oath. Three days after they had made the treaty with the Gibeonites, the Israelites heard that they were neighbors.

The Israelites were duped because they thought they knew the truth—they went by appearances and believed lies because they failed to inquire of the Lord. Will God give us wisdom and insight into matters we are not sure about? You bet he will! James states in the first chapter of his book, verse 5, "If any of you lacks wisdom, you should ask God, who gives generously to all without finding fault, and it will be given to you." The key, of course, is to ask. James also points out, "You do not have because you do not ask God" (James 4:2).

Being a Disciple Who Prays Effectively

We know that the disciples were intrigued by Jesus's prayer life because they asked Jesus to teach them to pray. This scenario is illustrated in Luke 11:1–4:

One day Jesus was praying in a certain place. When he finished, one of his disciples said to him, "Lord, teach us to pray, just as John taught his disciples." He said to them, "When you pray, say, 'Father, hallowed be your name, your kingdom come. Give us each day our daily bread. Forgive our sins, for we forgive everyone who sins against us. And lead us not into temptation.'"

Jesus taught them *what* to pray. Notice what happened next. Jesus then taught them *how* to pray. According to Luke 11:5–8,

> *Then Jesus said to them, "Suppose you have a friend, and you go to him at midnight and say, 'Friend, lend me three loaves of bread; a friend of mine on a journey has come to me, and I have no food to offer him.' And suppose the one inside answers, 'Don't bother me. The door is already locked, and my children and I are in bed. I can't get up and give you anything.' I tell you, even though he will not get up and give you the bread because of friendship, yet because of your shameless audacity he will surely get up and give you all you need."*

"Shameless audacity"? What is that? The words that immediately come to mind for me are "reckless abandon." The Amplified version of the New Testament renders Luke 11:8 as, "yet because of his persistence and boldness . . ."

We have the "what" to pray, and now we have the "how." But Jesus wasn't finished. Oh no, he punctuates these points by adding two other important nuances he does not want us to miss. The first is found in verse 9 and 10: "So I say to you: Ask and it will be given to you; seek and you will find; knock and the door will be opened to you. For everyone who asks receives; the one who seeks finds; and to the one who knocks, the door will be opened."

Jesus specifies three additional ways to pray: ask, seek, and knock. These are repetitive with slight differences. To ask is to make a request; to seek is to continue on a journey of discovery; and to knock implies that we identify a door that we know has the answer on the other side, a door that will surely be opened as we continue to knock.

Then Jesus points to the next element, God's character. Luke 11:11–13: "Which of you fathers, if your son asks for a fish, will give him a snake instead? Or if he asks for an egg, will he give him a scorpion? If you then, though you are evil, know how to give good gifts to your children, how much more will your Father in heaven give the Holy Spirit to those who ask him!"

In other words, we have the needed information on what to pray, how to pray, the ways to persist, and the character of the Father in heaven, who longs to give good things to us, his children. In Mathew 7:9–11 Jesus says the same thing in a slightly different way, exchanging "Holy Spirit" for the words "good gifts." God gives us the "good things" by giving us the Holy Spirit—in other words, himself—with his power, presence, and wisdom. We receive immeasurably by asking, seeking, and knocking. So then, how do our prayers work? How does God receive our prayers, and what does he do with them?

There is a beautiful picture in Revelation 5:7–8 that clarifies what happens with our prayers. Jesus "went and took the scroll from the right hand of him who sat on the throne. And when he had taken it, the four living creatures and the twenty-four elders fell down before the Lamb. Each one had a harp and they were holding golden bowls full of incense, *which are the prayers of God's people*" (emphasis added).

Do you understand the significance of the scene in heaven? Our prayers— the prayers of the saints, for that is who we are—fill golden bowls and become incense, a sweet fragrance before the Lord of heaven. Our prayers ascend upward, and he receives them! More prayer, more incense, more effect in heaven and more effect on the earth as the Lord receives more and more of that prayer incense and responds. This is an amazing truth depicting how precious and powerful our prayers really are: they are incense before the very throne of God in heaven! We need to persist in prayer as Jesus taught us because our prayers are getting through! So, don't stop . . . don't quit! They continue to expand, and their sweetness permeates the throne room of God!

How can you as a disciple grow in this opportunity to pray? First, it is advisable to simply get off on your own and begin to speak out whatever is on your heart and mind to the Lord. Your wording and ability to articulate are not issues with the Lord, nor is your perspective on your worthiness to approach him. We delight in the babble of an infant and encourage it in sometimes embarrassing ways! How much more does our Father in heaven relish hearing from you and me?

There are a few basic ways to approach praying to the Father. First, there is spontaneous prayer, speaking to God about whatever comes to mind. In essence, this is trusting that what you are thinking about is what the Lord wants you to pray about and what you need to pray about.

Sometimes we can become overly "religious" and premeditated in our praying. Spontaneous prayer is very freeing in that we can pray about any- thing, or anyone, at any time. When something comes to mind, pray about it. When someone comes to mind, pray for them.

Prayer can also be done with a list. This allows you to write down those pressing things to which you want to return time and again. This helps you to remember what you want to pray about. There are prayer apps that have been developed that allow you to list various praises, petitions, requests, and intercessions. Some apps will even send you reminders to pray. Because of our busy schedules, this can be helpful.

Another very effective way to pray is with a model to follow. The best model I used early on, which is still a pattern I quite often follow, is based on the acronym ACTS. The ACTS prayer model follows the Lord's prayer in its progression. When Jesus's disciples came to him and asked them to teach them to pray, he responded in Matthew 6:9–13, "This, then, is how you should pray: 'Our Father in heaven, hallowed be your name, your kingdom come, your will be done, on earth as it is in heaven. Give us today our daily bread. And forgive us our debts, as we also have forgiven our debtors. And lead us not into temptation, but deliver us from the evil one.'"

The ACTS model follows the sequence of Jesus's prayer, and the letter prompts stand for:

A = Adoration
C = Confession
T = Thanksgiving
S = Supplication (meaning "ask")

In other words, you begin praying by offering *adoration*, praise, and worship. This is simply acknowledging to God, as Jesus did at the opening of his prayer, that he is holy. You can add many other statements of God's attributes: e.g., that God is magnificent, he is powerful, he is perfect, he is good, he is loving, and he is faithful. Let's put that in the first person, so it reads like what you would pray. "Heavenly Father, you are holy. Lord, you are magnificent, and you are perfect and loving. God, you are faithful, and, Lord, I know you are a rescuer every day of my life."

You can add so much more. The psalms offer great truths to pray about and to use in giving praise to the Lord. For example, you could pray based on the words of Psalm 150:

Praise the Lord. Praise God in his sanctuary; praise him in his mighty heavens. Praise him for his acts of power; praise him for his surpassing greatness. Praise him with the sounding of the trumpet, praise him with the harp and lyre, praise him with timbrel and dancing, praise him with the strings and pipe, praise him with the clash of cymbals, praise him with resounding cymbals. Let everything that has breath praise the Lord. Praise the Lord.

Another Scripture-based praise is from Revelation 5:12–13:

"Worthy is the Lamb, who was slain, to receive power and wealth and wisdom and strength and honor and praise!" Then I heard every creature in heaven and on earth and under the earth and on the sea, and all that is in them, saying: "To him who sits on the throne and to the Lamb be praise and honor and glory and power, for ever and ever!":23-24

The next element in the Lord's prayer is *confession*. This is a vital part of praying, as we all deal with sins and faults in our lives. Be honest with the Lord. He already knows everything about your life! You can come to him without shame, regret, or embarrassment.

When my kids were young, every now and then one would approach my wife with a story of something they had done that they knew was wrong. Their honest, heartfelt confession drew compassion and mercy from her as a parent. She would relate these special moments when I would return from a day of teaching. I was always moved and challenged by the ways in which she showed grace and compassion to our children.

We love our kids. God loves his kids. God loves you. Tell him what is on your heart and mind. If you are not quite sure, ask him to show you if there is anything getting in the way of your relationship with him. David the Psalmist wrote, "Search me, God, and know my heart; test me and know my anxious thoughts. See if there is any offensive way in me, and lead me in the way everlasting" (Psalm 139:23, 24).

Whenever I have entered into a time of prayer and made this request, quieted my heart, and waited, something has come to mind. I then confess it to the Lord, thank him for his forgiveness, and continue praying. If I receive from him no other word in response, I thank him for the peace he gives and move on. God wants clear communication with us. Have you ever had someone do something that bothered you and misused your friendship? Then you know the barrier this can bring about between the two of you that can only be resolved by an honest talk. When that happens and forgiveness is offered, all is well again, and there is such a feeling of freshness!

The Lord prods us with a gentle conviction about matters we need to take care of. He is never harsh or demeaning and never condemns. He gently urges, gently nudges us in the direction of freedom. Sin brings shame, guilt, and even bondage. In contrast, Jesus announced, "I have come that they may have life, and have it to the full!" (John 10:10). And again, "So if the Son sets you free, you will be free indeed!" (John 8:36). As John the apostle wrote, "If we confess our sins, he is faithful and just and will forgive us our sins and purify us from all unrighteousness" (1 John 1:9).

Take time with your confession before the Lord. There have been times when I have confessed things to him that have brought me to tears. I stay in that posture, knowing that the Lord receives my confession, and I feel his lovingkindness envelop me and reassure me that no sin can separate me from him and that his love is secure—as is his great power to foster within me growth and strength in him.

Discipleship is a process of growth, and the Lord is committed to leading us through our own issues and mistakes. It didn't bother him to take and use Moses, who had committed murder, as well as Paul the apostle, who was guilty of consenting to the same, or Mary, a woman who had been possessed by demons; he was happy to call these and other flawed individuals as those he would lead through the issues of their past to become true disciples who would live and even, in some cases, die for him. God can and will do the same for you. No matter what your past, no matter what your tendencies, confess them to the Father, knowing that he is faithful and just to forgive your sins and lead you into all righteousness.

After confession comes *thanksgiving*. It is vital to express your gratitude to the Lord. What do you thank him for? First, thank him for who he is! God is good in every way. He saves us through faith in the cross of Jesus Christ, through whose resurrection we receive the power to live. Consider all the ways he has been good to you, provided for you, rescued you, delivered you, healed you, and sustained you.

Beyond the litany of what he has done for you is the very fact that you are his child. Thank him for his incredible love for you and for bringing you into his family! If you are in a vibrant church family, thank him for the blessing of growing alongside brothers and sisters and being cared for by pastors who shepherd and teach you so you continually grow in Christ. You can also thank him for the tests and trials that draw you close to him and teach you strength and endurance.

There is an important truth about the act of thanksgiving you need to understand. Thanksgiving is the offering we give to the Lord that ushers us into his presence. In Psalm 100:4 the psalmist implores us to "enter into his gates with thanksgiving." The picture in this psalm is of the congregation of Israel singing aloud together as they enter in unity through the gates to the temple, approaching the place where they will experience the presence of God.

When we give thanks to the Lord, that expression offers us the same experience—to walk into the place where God dwells and to experience him. I have learned over the years that, when my faith is flat or I am in a funk and there seems to be no spiritual vitality, when I begin to thank the Lord and make that list grow, speaking to him about who he is and what he has done, I once again sense his Spirit and recognize that the act of thanksgiving has ushered me into his presence.

Thankfulness is an interesting phenomenon that science has shown makes a massive impact on our whole system. People who practice thankfulness tend to have less anxiety, less disease, longer and more enjoyable lives, better work experiences, and better relationships.[4] God has given us a mechanism that is wonderful and powerful! Thankfulness gets God's attention. It tells him that we recognize his goodness and faithfulness.

I'm sure you like getting a compliment every now and then. Think of what a genuine compliment does for you—it makes you beam on the inside. It is like food for your soul. When we thank the Lord, we are going beyond just complimenting him—we are truly looking at our Father and telling him how much we appreciate who he is in his character.

The final element in the ACTS prayer model is *supplication*, which is the action of asking. We have earlier covered the ways to ask, but this important issue bears a reminder. When it comes to supplication, there is the definite pursuit of what you are requesting by asking, seeking, and knocking. This is the time to ask the Lord for all things personal, relational, physical, and financial . . . and you can add to the list. What you pray about is what God responds to. So, ask!

Again, continue to bring your requests to God. And remember the promises of God in response to your requests: "This is the confidence we have in approaching God: that if we ask anything according to his will, he hears us. And if we know that he hears us—whatever we ask—we know we have what we asked of him" (1 John 5:14, 15).

The apostle Paul gives us great encouragement to pray we he writes, "Now to Him who is able to do exceedingly abundantly above all we ask or think . . ." (Ephesians 3:20 NKJV). Notice that God does "exceedingly abundantly." Consider those two terms placed together by this wise apostle. "Exceedingly" means beyond our expectations. To exceed is to excel, to take further, to go beyond. "Abundantly" means in a large, and even excessive quantity—more than enough! Taken together, Paul is letting us know that God will answer in ways that are not only beyond our expectations but in overflowing quantity. So, keep expecting these types of answers as you continue praying!

Have you ever heard the acronym PUSH? It means Pray Until Something Happens. Or how about this equation, spoken by many a preacher: Much prayer, much power. Little prayer, little power. No prayer, no power. (So, keep praying and receiving his power!) God is already at work to answer our supplications, and he loves for us to partner with him by asking for the answers to our prayers.

There is another aspect of prayer that is important for the disciple of Jesus Christ to learn: intercession. To intercede is to intervene on behalf of another. Intercession is a form of prayer that is generally denoted by the earnest, persistent asking and seeking of God. It is shown in Scripture on many occasions. A prime example is Jesus praying in John 17, asking the Father for protection for his disciples and for all who would one day follow him.

Another great picture of intercession is Abraham in Genesis 22:18–33. Because of the great wickedness in Sodom, God said he would destroy the city. He confided this to Abraham, who had family living there. Abraham interceded continually, asking the Lord to relent if there were 50 righteous people in Sodom. The Lord agreed. Then Abraham asked for God to relent if there were 45, then 40, then 30, then 20, and then finally only 10. With each new request from Abraham, God responded in the affirmative. Abraham did not settle for what he had already heard but pressed in and continued to bravely ask again, requesting something more audacious each time.

One of the most intense biblical pictures of intercession is Moses before God, asking the Lord to part the waters of the Red Sea, to provide food, and to forgive the Israelites when they rebelled on many occasions. Moses's prayer, recounted in Deuteronomy 9, is the testimony of Israel rebelling against God, the Lord telling Moses that he would destroy them, and then Moses's humble intercession: "Then once again I fell prostrate before the LORD for forty days and forty nights; I ate no bread and drank no water, because of all the sin you had committed, doing what was evil in the LORD's sight and so arousing his anger. I feared the anger and wrath of the LORD, for he was angry enough with you to destroy you. But again, the LORD listened to me" (Deuteronomy 9:18, 19).

Intercession is a serious form of seeking the Lord, with a more intense focus, usually for a longer period of time. While the biblical examples here depict forms of intercession, intercessory prayer is shown to have been a common practice in both the Old and New Testaments. It is still an important practice for Christians all over the world. This should become a regular practice for a disciple who is serious about seeing things change in their own lives and in the lives of others, the nation, and the world.

Prayer is vital. Sometimes it is natural and flows easily from our hearts and lips. However, sometimes prayer is work. The practice of prayer definitely requires a daily investment in time and focus. We are being engaged in battle by hell itself when it comes to prayer, so we shouldn't be surprised by the attacks and distractions that come when we try to pray. It goes with the territory.

By the way, just an anecdote here. When you are distracted, tempted strongly, or foggy in your thinking, it is usually because you need to pray about something, and the messengers of Satan are trying to keep you from that assignment. Can the enemy read your mind or know your thoughts? No. He is limited. However, the powers of hell do see the work that heaven is doing and your involvement in that work. They know when angels are dispatched from the presence of God to come to help, and they fight those winged messengers.

Read Daniel 10 about the fight between an angel of God and a demonic spirit. This is a spiritual reality. We *must* keep up the work of prayer. Heaven is depending on us, as are those around us, and the church body needs our intercession. Be that warrior who commits to prayer and stays with the task. The rewards now and through eternity will be incredible!

In addition to prayer with intercession is the discipline of fasting. I am placing the practice of fasting within the context of prayer because they generally work together, as Jesus pointed out in Matthew 7:21.

What is fasting? Fasting is the practice of setting aside some form of food or foregoing some meals to focus on God's purposes. The Lord responds to sacrifice, as is shown in the sacrifice of his Son, Jesus. Sacrifice is blessed by God. When we set aside something that is needed for our daily sustenance, God intervenes by his Spirit, responding in a variety of powerful ways.

First, a spiritual blessing is bestowed. Prayer is answered. This is shown in Daniel's fasting and continued prayer before the Lord in Daniel 10. Jesus also taught this principle to his disciples after he had cast out a demon from a child when they could not. His words were, "This kind does not go out except by prayer and fasting" (Matthew 17:21 NKJV).

Fasting can be the self-denial of certain foods, as Daniel exemplified in Daniel 10. Fasting can be for periods of days or, as Jesus and Moses did, for as long as forty days. I believe it is beneficial to start small and learn to grow in the practice of fasting over time. I do think it is valuable for true disciples to develop a discipline of fasting and learn how the Lord opens up our spiritual ears while we fast, breaking chains and providing answers to prayers in ways that are new and marvelous.

When I first learned about fasting, it was through my affiliation with Athletes in Action, an arm of Campus Crusade for Christ. Dr. Bill Bright, the Campus Crusade founder, had written about fasting and his journey with it. I was intrigued. Along with that, I remember listening to a national leader on his radio program talking about his godly grandfather deciding to forgo breakfast and waiting until lunch to eat in order to spend more time in prayer one day per week.

On that day he would take his Bible to lunch, read, and pray for his family—his kids and grandkids. Then he moved on to two days a week. I thought to myself, *I think I could try that one day per week.* So, I began. I was starting a new teaching position and coaching a middle school wrestling team. During that season I recognized open doors with the wrestlers I had never noticed before. Kids were asking questions. Conversations occurred. I am not sure how many of the boys began to follow Jesus Christ that year, but there were several—and they are still following Jesus to this day—over thirty years later.

One morning per week. God challenged me, and I accepted the challenge. He knew what he was doing—getting me to sacrifice something small to gain something immeasurable. What is God challenging you to do right now?

Chapter 6

Being a Disciple Who Is a Natural Witness

A witness in court testifies about what they have seen and heard about a particular person or situation, telling what they know to be true. For the disciple of Jesus Christ, the greatest opportunity is to be a witness about Jesus! When I think about my testimony, I think of what I was like before I began to follow Jesus, what the circumstances were that surrounded my decision to follow Jesus, and what difference was made by my initial decision to follow him. Although I wrote about my decision to follow Jesus Christ earlier on, there is another testimony I have to offer—one that has fueled my desire to be a witness for Jesus Christ.

When my oldest son, Jordan, was ten years old, we were part of a church that put together a fantastic kids' program that focused on teaching biblical principles using the alphabet with rhymes and songs. It caught on quite well, and our pastor was asked to bring this program and our team to the denomination's summer camp. We were tasked with leading the children's ministry, which involved hundreds of kids from around the state.

There was a group of a dozen kids from an inner-city mission who proved to be quite a handful. Every day at the end of the kids' program, which ended at noon for lunch, we offered a time of prayer, during which we invited kids to raise their hand if they wanted to begin a relationship with Jesus Christ. We were excited to see many kids choose to follow Christ each day, and every day one or two kids from the mission would raise their hands to have someone pray with them.

Then there was Robert, the ringleader of this group of kids. Although he had an immense cherubic smile, it was usually seen after he had led some small but outlandish prank or activity during the services. This was frustrating, to be sure, but it was hard to be upset when he would flash that cheesy grin.

Every morning before the service our team prayed together for the different activities and talks to display God's love, asking that kids would want to begin a relationship with Jesus Christ. And every day we prayed specifically for Robert. Each morning we prayed harder, especially as we neared Friday, the last day of camp. On that day we had all our engines revving. We were prayed up, excited, and gave it our all. After the program, when prayer time began, many more hands went up . . . but not Robert's.

Our team was on the verge of disappointment when, at the very end of the prayer time, one small hand slowly went up. It was Robert's! Jordan and a couple of kids and an adult on our team hustled over—and found Robert in tears. He wanted prayer for his mother . . . and for himself, to know Jesus. Soon the entire group was gathered around, praying quietly as Robert prayed to begin a relationship with Jesus. We sat with him and encouraged him for a while, along with his friends. When we all left for lunch, there were smiles of joy, praises, and thankfulness for the breakthrough in Robert and so many other kids.

As we sat at lunch, our team was exhausted, yet relieved for the week and its activities to be almost over. Suddenly the camp siren sounded. The siren went off only if there was a problem at the lake. We all ran to the water, where there was a large ladder and platform for jumping into the water onto a large tube called the Blob. Some of the kids had snuck out of lunch, gone over the fence, and gone swimming when the lake was closed.

On the dock that led to the ladders was one of our adults, a doctor, hunched over on the dock performing mouth-to-mouth resuscitation on a boy. He stopped and traded off with another doctor, but, after several minutes, they both stopped—it was too late. It was apparent that the boy had drowned, and they couldn't revive him. As we looked more closely, we realized that the boy was Robert. We were in shock, stunned and broken.

Robert and his friends had wanted one last splash in the water before returning home. Robert apparently had jumped off the highest ladder onto the tube, slipped off, and been unable to get back up. His friends had run to get help . . . but he had been under the water too long.

That evening our team met to try to gain some semblance of understanding before returning home. We sat together and cried. Some were angry. "Why, God? How could this happen? Robert had just begun a brand new life. Why such a disaster? What happens now? How can there be such pain after such an effort to minister to kids for you?" Honest questions from hurting servants.

Then one of the teens from our group stood up and said, "When I went back to my room after we left the lake this afternoon, I lay on my bed in unbelievable pain and just cried. All of a sudden, I had a vision in my head as I lay there. I saw myself at the water's edge. While Doc was working on Robert, I saw something whisk out of Robert's body—it was his soul—looking just like Robert, with the biggest smile on his face you could imagine. He started to fly upward with his arms outstretched and his eyes gazing forward.

"I followed his gaze and saw Jesus, with a huge smile, there in the sky coming toward Robert with his arms reaching out. He grabbed him, and up and away, heavenward, they went. I realized that, had we not been at that camp at this time, praying and believing for Robert, that scene might never have happened. We were supposed to be here today so that Robert could know Jesus before he left this planet."

There was silence in the room. Then tears, after which spontaneous prayer broke out and praises to a Father whose ways are beyond our understanding. Through mixed tears we shared more praises; worship; and finally, prayers for what God would have us do next. I was freshly encouraged but also freshly chastised. You see, when I had been invited to take part with this team, I had fought it for a while. Did I really want to devote an entire week of my summer for a kids' camp? I mean, I already teach kids nine months of the year, I coach, and I have other places I might like to go on vacation. I fought it but finally and reluctantly gave in. Now, standing with these brothers and sisters, fully enveloped in the Lord's work and all that had just occurred, I was ashamed of my previous attitude and my own selfishness.

I thought about that picture of Robert and my young teammate's words, and a verse came to mind from Revelation, the last book of the Bible: "He will wipe every tear from their eyes" (Revelation 21:4). I had often wondered about that verse, but now it came to mind on the tail end of everything we had just experienced. What could that mean? God will wipe away sorrow? Pain? Regrets? Will the tears be of joy for the grand entrance into heaven, a heaven we don't deserve but our entry into which has been paid in full by the blood of the One who is the lamp of heaven—Jesus himself?

Then a reality hit me. I suddenly envisioned the Lord replaying a tape of my life before me one day in heaven. I know that we will receive rewards and our dead works will be burned up (1 Corinthians 3:15). But I was startled by this view of myself, at seeing my life revealed—all of it, including all of the opportunities God had set up for me to witness for him in life, to tell someone about Jesus or to help someone in trouble or to give of my abundance to someone in need or to go on a ministry trip . . . including the many times I had let the oppor-tunities slip by. I didn't help because I was too busy, too afraid, or too apathetic.

Then I began to weep. And I began to understand that those tears might be the ones I will cry because of my refusal to witness for him. Incredibly, he will afterward, as a loving Father, wipe those tears from my eyes.

That night I faded off to sleep but had, for the second time in my life, a very spiritual dream. In my dream I was an active, comfortable, successful businessman. I was happy and healthy and had a loving family. Suddenly I found myself in an expansive area with vast clouds around me. I wondered if it was heaven and then surmised that I had died and was standing in heaven, alone but curious. From the far distance a man came walking toward me with a great sea of people following him closely.

He walked straight up to me with an expressive, beaming smile and exclaimed, "Welcome, brother! What brought you here?" I thought for a second and replied, "I don't know—I think I had a heart attack, maybe?" Then, as he looked around me, as if to find someone there, he added, "Who have you brought with you?" I looked around me and saw no one. "I don't think anyone . . . but my family, one day, hopefully . . . Who are all of these with you?" (There looked to be thousands with him, as far as I could tell.)

"These are the ones," he joyfully replied, "who believed because of my testimony! I am from Asia and shared my testimony in spite of many warnings and imprisonments. I was tortured for my belief in Jesus my Savior, but these with me, they saw and believed, and here we are!"

I awoke from this dream, sat up in bed, and wept afresh. I would not, could not go another day in my life waffling between two worlds. I made a decision—to put a stake in the ground. "Lord Jesus," I said through my tears, "I will spend every day of the rest of my life looking for every opportunity to witness for you and to share your great name. Give me more opportunities, Lord. I want to see heaven populated—I want to offer you what my Asian friend offered to you—people! As gifts for you! You deserve nothing less. I want there to be thousands with me one day as I stand before you—as an offering to you, Lord Jesus! You are worthy of it all!"

This event solidified for me the desire to be a witness at all times, in every place, through any means. This was my wake-up call to be a witness. I pray that you, too, may have a heart sold out to Jesus Christ to be his witness wherever you go.

What will you offer him one day in his presence?

What will you spend your life pursuing?

To Be a Disciple Is to Be a Witness Who Cares

The way to be a witness is to recognize, first, that you are called to be one, but more than just a witness—a disciple-maker. Look at Matthew 28:19, 20: "Go and make disciples of all nations, baptizing them in the name of the Father and of the Son and of the Holy Spirit, and teaching them to obey everything I have commanded you."

To make disciples requires sharing your faith.

A young man I mentor asked me recently, "What does it take to witness . . . You know, to share your faith with someone?"

Great question.

My response was, "I think you need two things. The first is to love people and to actually care about them. The second is curiosity. Love makes you care about a person. You value them because God, who designed them, loves them intimately and wants them to know him intimately. Curiosity is that childlike, joyful attitude that causes you to ask questions and then to ask more questions, which leads to discovery and a shared experience. That, to me, is witnessing. This can take place with a long-standing relationship, a relative, a new acquaintance, or someone you interact with at the gas station, a restaurant, or on the phone.

My friend, this is something you should consider, pray about, and pray for. Consider what it means to love. Do you really love people? If not, why not? There is a paradigm shift that needs to take place in our heads and then our hearts if we struggle to truly love people the way God loves them. And trust me, he sees everything about them—infinitely more than we do. To help with this, read Luke 15. In this provocative chapter Jesus uses three profound stories to reveal his Father's insatiable love for people. In this scenario, Jesus is speaking to a diverse group of "sinners" and Pharisees. While we know that they were all sinful people, regardless of position, some acknowledged that they were, while the others were carefully hiding their sins.

The stories tell of lost things: a lost sheep, a lost coin, and a lost son. Here is the clincher: Jesus was digging in deeply to show how incredible God's true character is, as shown by his loving in ways that are actually audacious and, to be honest, even embarrassing. The "sinners" gathered there must have been gleeful to hear of God as a Father who would leave the flock to find them, toss everything around in the house searching for them, and forgive completely to get them back. The religious crowd, the Pharisees on hand, would have sneered at such audacious actions.

Why would a shepherd leave the wealth of ninety-nine healthy sheep to search in dangerous places for one sheep with a tendency to wander off? Who would ever see the sinners before them as valued coins and, again, disrupt all of life to find one? Move on with the ones who are available, most would say! And what self-respecting father would embarrass himself by lifting up his garments and running recklessly after a kid who deserved the chastisement and banishment of the village?

This last tale was preposterous! Yet Jesus subtly pleaded with his listeners, referring to these religious fakes through the image of the older son—merciless, yet himself needing mercy. Cold, unforgiving, yet needing the warmth of the forgiveness of God himself. And, oh, the "sinners." Can you picture them delighting in the offer of the love of a Father who would chase them down and welcome them in, bestowing on them sonship and a place in the heavenly family with forgiveness, acceptance, and value?

We bear witness to what we have received and experienced—telling about the kind of Father who loves in the way Jesus depicted—with every category of sinful person coming to hear him tell the tales of the Father's great love for them and the ways God would reach out to them.

What is the story your life tells? What is the story you long to tell? Is it about the love of a Father who has saved you and continues to pursue you, showing you his love day after day in more ways than you can count? There is a world around us that needs our stories of Jesus's love and saving grace. There is a world around you that needs to hear your story of Jesus's love and saving grace!

Chapter 7

Being a Disciple Who Is Filled Up in Order to Be Poured Out

During one of Jesus's journeys he spoke to a Samaritan woman at a well. Samaritans were looked down upon by the Jews as lower class. In John 4 Jesus asked the Samaritan woman if she would give him a drink. She was perplexed why this Jewish man would stoop to ask her a question, being that she was considered lower class, not to mention a woman. Jesus said to her, "If you knew the gift of God and who asks you for a drink, you would have asked him and he would have given you *living water.*" He was referring to the water of life, the Holy Spirit.

Jesus was always ready to tell about the Father, the Holy Spirit, and himself as the One sent by his Father. The water, the Holy Spirit, is what Jesus had and what he offered to this Samaritan woman. Actually, he offers that Holy Spirit drenching to all of us. The apostle Paul emphasized this for all believers as he wrote to the Ephesian Christians, "Do not get drunk on wine, which leads to debauchery. Instead, *be filled with the Spirit*" (Ephesians 5:18, emphasis added). The Greek word for "be filled" is *pleroo,*[5] meaning to the brim, in abundant supply, in an ongoing manner.

How can we be ready to be poured out, to be used by the Lord in any and every situation? We must be filled with the Spirit of God, daily saturated with truth and worship. This brings about the movement of God in us, which readies us for the interactions God has set up for us. I love this truth: "For we are God's handiwork, created in Christ Jesus to do good works, which God prepared in advance for us to do" (Ephesians 2:10).

Isn't that incredible? Before the foundation of the world, God set up activities, interactions, and occurrences with you in mind! He prepared situations for you to enter so that you could use your particular giftings and personality to influence and impact the lives of people around you. You've been set up . . . for success! God intends for you to enter into those prede-termined situations, knowing that *he* is with you and will guide you through.

Yet, as with all things in our relationship with the Father, he offers a part-nership. In other words, he prepared the situations and invites you to prepare yourself for them. Our preparation is staying in the Word of God, being faith-ful in prayer, continuing to worship the Lord, and having God's purposes as our first priority. God wants you to do well in your home, in school, on your job, or in that sport you love. And he wants you there for a greater purpose than just raising a family, getting successful grades, earning a wage or sal-ary, or gaining competitive success.

He wants you to be there as a witness for Jesus Christ. The best way to wit-ness is from a heart that wants to witness because you have experienced the presence and truth of God and have within you the fullness of God—being saturated by it through the Word, prayer, and worship. These aren't strategies but experiences. They are moments you enter by deciding each new day that whatever God has for you as a loving Father is more enticing, more personal, and more rejuvenating than anything else out there.

In our current Western church culture, we Christians subscribe to many business practices. I'm not saying that this is either right or wrong. I am trying to point out, however, that we can tend to be transactional in our relation-ships, including our relationship with God. If you are the type of person who "checks the boxes"—you know, completes one task and moves on to the next thing—then you will not only miss the center point of your relationship with Jesus Christ but may relate to the Christian message as transactional. Your paradigm may be something like: God did this for me, so my response is . . . It would be tragic to relate an intimate relationship with Jesus as a transaction, and this would provide so much less than God intends.

My friend, dive in. You are welcomed, you are invited, and you are searched out and beckoned by the Spirit of God to immerse yourself in wor-ship, prayer, and a deepening love for the Word of God that will enable you to give an answer to anyone who asks about the hope you have in Jesus Christ (1 Peter 3:15). He is the living water—and we get to be filled by that water, to then pour it out into the lives of others!

To Be a Disciple Is to Build Bridges to Others

What does it look like to build a bridge to someone else?

My daughter, Lauren, and I were walking in the mall near us and stopped at a favorite spot: Auntie Anne's Pretzels. We love the cinnamon sugar pretzels. The smell alone is enough to draw me from any region of the mall, beckoned along by the siren-like aroma. As we ordered our usual treats, the young girl across the counter reached out her hand to take my credit card. I noticed a tattoo that I had not seen before, so I asked, "Could I ask you about your tattoo?"

The young lady replied, "Yes—it means my life almost stopped, but then it went on again. I decided to live. Now I am trying to learn what I am here for." I asked next if she had yet found that answer. She replied that she had not found out yet but was waiting and praying to know what her purpose was. I asked if I could give her a thought along those lines, maybe to help. She gladly said, "Yes—I'd like to hear anything about my purpose."

I explained that I believed she was alive to learn what it means to be loved by a perfect Father who wanted her to know *him* . . . to learn his heart for her as a precious daughter, cared for and planned for before the world was formed and possessing honor, dignity, and beauty. Her eyes misted up as she received those words.

She stated that she wanted to know what the love of a father was really like. We listened to her unlock her heart a bit more. I knew we had limited time, so I asked if I could pray for her. My daughter moved in close while this precious young lady took my hand from across the counter. My daughter put her hand into ours, and I prayed that this young lady would receive the love of God—the love of a Father—and learn that the Father had created her for purpose and beauty; to see the world as he sees it; to see herself as he sees her; and to experience forgiveness, love, and life in Jesus Christ. As we parted, she had a wonderful smile on her face. Lauren and I prayed that God would lead this precious girl to more of himself.

Building bridges with people involves loving them because the Father loves them and wants us to introduce him to them. Building bridges involves looking for what is common between you and another person and what makes you curious. Building bridges necessitates being observant—noticing what God wants you to see in a person. They may have a style of hair or clothing that stands out, a pet, a tattoo, a piece of jewelry, or something else that catches your eye. The key is that they have already caught the Father's eye, and we get to tell them that—provided we are patient, careful, affirming, loving, and interested. Sometimes, even in the crazy age we live in, people will let us in.

Proverbs 20:5 (GNT) offers keen insight for building bridges to people: "A person's thoughts are like water in a deep well, but someone with insight can draw them out." Insight begins with caring enough to notice what is unique and special about someone and then being curious and brave enough to ask. What do you ask? Polite, general, nonthreatening questions. There may be a story attached to them. We all have stories and like to tell them.

What is one recurring story you tell about yourself? I have several go-to stories nowadays—as my wife and kids will tell you; they have heard them all! Most of us are quick to share *what* we do. I like to tell people I am a retired teacher and that I now oversee a ministry called 99:1. If someone pursues that, asking about 99:1 Ministries, I let them know that I help people by counseling, teaching, encouraging, and coming alongside them to help them grow in whatever areas they need. I make my time available for meeting with people in whatever setting they need. I don't spend much time on my own story because I really want to hear from the person I am talking with. Still, sometimes our stories merge, and that leads to more conversation. More often than not someone tells me what they do, who they are, or what is happening in their life.

The key to making the conversation effective is to ask another question. For example, if someone tells me about the work they do, I'll ask them if they like it. This can lead to so much more. Likewise, if someone talks about their family, I'll ask what the kids are into—sports, school, and ages—that sort of thing. If I am talking with an older person, we usually discuss how long they've been married, their work or career, their family, and their hopes for the future.

If in any response I hear something that could be pursued, I ask about it. I simply ask another question. But you know what? I *want* to know the answer. Why? Because I care about the person I am talking with, whether a new acquaintance, a close friend, or someone across a counter at a place of business. They really matter to God, and so, they really matter to me. People need to matter to us.

What does it take for a Father to look at this lost and broken world and hurt so much for the people who are lost and broken that he would send his Son—his one and only son—to live and die for each and every one? I believe in the Scriptures, we are introduced to a Father who loves us to extreme levels that we can neither define nor deny.

So then, witnessing or sharing Christ with someone, it would seem to me, is being delightfully interested in a person and wanting to know about them; it means caring about their life, their triumphs, their failures, their hopes, their dreams, and trying to find a way to let them know how much they matter to God. My thought is, *If I care about them and really listen, will they somehow* see that God the Father really listens and really cares? I hope so—I pray so—and I believe so.

One more thought here. It is vital, in being a witness, to ask questions and listen carefully. Remember, the message isn't about you as much as it is about the one you are talking with. If you get a chance to tell your story, great; however, that should always be secondary, as the time you spend is about the story of the person you are sharing with, about how the Father wants to show them ways in which his story includes and completes their own.

Part Two

Being a Disciple-Maker:
Leading Others as They Follow Jesus

Chapter 8

To Be Called . . . Afresh and New

H ere is the call:

Then Jesus came to them and said, "All authority in heaven and on earth has been given to me. Therefore go and make disciples of all nations, baptizing them in the name of the Father and of the Son and of the Holy Spirit, and teaching them to obey everything I have commanded you." (Matthew 28:18–20)

You are called by Jesus himself to go and make disciples!

Part One has been all about being a disciple: how to walk, practice, and train to be a disciple who follows Jesus Christ. Part Two of this book focuses on how to make disciples. It offers suggestions on how you can foster that desire in your relationships and intentionally walk with others as someone who desires to obey the Lord's directive to make disciples.

Being a Disciple-Maker Who Heeds the Call

Make the decision now. Put a stake in the ground. Raise a banner. "I am a disciple-maker for the Lord Jesus Christ!" Don't ever leave the place to which God has called you: your commission is to call men and women, the young and the old, to follow Jesus Christ.

God has uniquely created you and shaped you through many life experiences to be a disciple-maker who will walk with those God has planned for you to walk with. Some of this will happen naturally, and some opportunities will come to light as you actively seek the Lord to discover those he wants you to walk with.

As a Disciple-Maker, You Need a Network of Faithful Friends

Three-Level Relationship

Someone over me, someone alongside me, someone I watch over. We need all of these types of people in our lives. Is there a scriptural precedent for this? Of course. When Paul first started to follow Jesus, he had Barnabas over him as a mentor for a number of years. Silas, Priscilla, and Aquilla walked alongside him (as well as many others of the apostles and faithful believers), and he had Timothy, as a spiritual son, to watch over.

In fact, Paul had many spiritual sons—Onesimus, Philemon, and John Mark, to name a few more. The same relationship structure can be found throughout the Old and New Testaments. When you think about this triple relationship element, it doesn't take long to notice the beauty, value, and reality of these tiers and to apply this principle in almost every walk of life.

In a family, the father and mother have or had parents over them. They walk together, alongside each other. They have brothers and sisters alongside them. They are over and offer oversight to their children. In the business world you may have a CEO. She or he may have a board that oversees them. The board and management team walk alongside the CEO. Yet the CEO is overseeing the employees, along with an administrative team.

The same is true in education and, especially, in the church. The church has pastors—overseers who watch over the members. The elders, called to come alongside the pastors, may also have collective oversight over them. In many cases there is also a denominational leadership over the church. This effective structure was in place already in the early church; think of James, the half brother of Jesus, who led in the first century. He was over the church, yet made decisions together with, and alongside, the apostles. They were over, or exercised oversight for, those who became believers in the Lord Jesus Christ.

Who is over you? Who is there in your life who is perhaps older or at least more experienced and hopefully wiser than you? If you know who that person is, do you regularly communicate with them? This is a vital safeguard. Quite frankly, you need that relationship in order to continue to foster your growth and, when necessary, correct your course. If you do not have someone in this capacity in your life, pray that the Lord will show you where this kind of relationship could take place.

Then actively look around you. There is probably someone waiting in the wings who simply needs to be asked, "Would it be okay to meet every now and then and just talk?" "Could we study the Bible together once a week?"

"Could I take you to coffee so we can talk about God?" I have found that the Lord has people waiting in the wings to serve his purposes. Again, pray and test the waters. There is nothing but a win that awaits you in this relationship . . . a win for both of you!

About fifteen years ago I noticed that an avalanche was occurring. While our Michigan weather holds many anomalies, and avalanches aren't in the mix naturally, yet it was clear that one was happening. It was spiritual. In our area of the US, there were a few well-known pastors who fell morally. On the national scene there were other, very notable pastors and Christian leaders who made terrible decisions and were removed or simply left their posts as shepherds of the flock of God. And, sadly, there were suicides in the leadership ranks.

To add to this, I had a couple of close friends who made life-changing choices that affected their ministries and families in devastating ways. One day as I was pondering all of this—the avalanche, as I refer to it—I looked up toward heaven and, from my guts, asked out loud, "Is this the end picture for the men and women in the church—devastation and ruin?"

I was hurting and felt utterly let down by all that was taking place. I instantaneously knew, however, that the fall of others did not signal a downward spiral for everyone. Each of us has opportunities to follow close to the Lord . . . but also to forsake our first love, Jesus Christ. I thought about that and wondered, *How then do I stay strong, or at least send out a flare when I am looking at potential trouble in my life?* I thought immediately of two answers: my wife, Anne, and brothers in the faith.

That evening I shocked my wife by saying, "Anne, I need you to begin to pray for me more. I feel vulnerable now in my life, more than at any other point." She looked worried and asked, "Is there something I should know . . . You have me a bit concerned . . . What do you mean?" I shared honestly with her that I was very disappointed in the way so many men had fallen or walked away from the calling Jesus had given them and in which they had once lived so victoriously. Now, for the first time in my life, I was recognizing how vulnerable I am—how vulnerable we all are—and I wanted to do something about it.

Immediately I reiterated that I *needed* her to pray for me more intentionally, to ask questions, and to observe my relationship with Christ and with our family. I had made some poor choices earlier in my Christian walk and in no way wanted to repeat any of my earlier mistakes. Second, I needed the closeness of brothers: men I could confide in, share life with, and rely on, as they could of me. I needed a band of brothers. I was quite sure that, if I needed others, they needed my support and friendship as well. While I have grown and learned to trust God, my wife, and close friends, I know that I am vulnerable and need people to whom I am accountable and in whom I can confide. I believe that we all need these friends and safeguards in our lives.

For the first time in my Christian life, I was learning that my strength was not enough. I had been an athlete my entire life. I was a wrestler and enjoyed running long distances as well. I had been all-state as a high schooler, All-American as a collegiate athlete, and had represented the United States overseas. I had competed in the Olympic Festival and Olympic trials tournaments. I knew what it was to train, to compete, to lose, and to win. But now, at this point in my life, none of that could bring about what I desired most—to live a life of commitment and obedience to Jesus Christ. For that to truly happen, I realized that I needed more help and more support than I ever had in the past. I had to seek out brothers who would want to walk closely with me, as I with them.

I did have one close friend I was meeting with on a weekly basis—Mike. We would read a book together, pray together, and talk about life and faith. This was a very sustaining and important relationship. I believe, in fact, that it is one of the most valuable friendships I have had. This has been a great mutual blessing for us as brothers, and we have relied on each other in many tough situations. While this was similar to what I was looking for, and certainly a deep relationship for both of us, I knew that I needed more than just one close friend. I felt as though I needed troops—a garrison. If I were going to flourish, and if others were going to flourish, there had to be more.

I began to pray and ask the Lord to show me who I should talk with about a mutual accountability relationship. I sought out one of the elders of my church—a man I respected and counted as a friend. He agreed that meeting together to support and challenge each other was a great idea that he had considered as well. We set up regular meetings every other week to talk, check on each other, and pursue godly disciplines—reading the Word of God, discussing spiritual truths, and taking seriously our roles as husbands and fathers.

It began well, but it didn't take long to see that our meetings were not moving beyond the surface. We had many meetings rescheduled due to time conflicts, and it seemed apparent that we just didn't have a mutual pursuit of God and each other as those who would walk together deeply. Maybe we were not ready for that level of commitment, or we just didn't know how to handle this at that time.

Our meetings dwindled and fizzled out after several months. Yet I knew there had to be more brothers like Mike and myself—perhaps many—who desired what I desired. Men who wanted to forge a friendship and walk together in a relationship of trust, honesty, and unbiased support. I especially longed for an older man to walk with me as a mentor.

In my earlier days as a believer, I had in my life a man I call Papaw—he was a true man of God who loved me dearly and made a big impact on me as a mentor, but Papaw lived in another state, so I didn't see him very often. I prayed and searched.

Then I met Loren.

At that point in my journey, I was on staff at my church as a Director of Spiritual Development. I also taught on many occasions. A pastor friend was part of a large church that had started an annual men's conference. He asked me to speak on the last night of the conference about spiritual formation. He added that there would be someone else there who would speak just after me on that last night.

This was an interesting arrangement, and I agreed. The conference was challenging but also a lot of fun. The last night was a Saturday. As is often the custom, we met backstage to do our run-through of what the night would look like. The stage crew and worship team, along with the pastor who had organized the event, were all there leading us through the setup for the last night, as well as the organization and sequence of events.

That is when my pastor friend introduced me to the man who would follow up after my teaching. It was going to be a sort of "one-two punch" of teaching and a time for the men to respond on this, the last night of the conference. So, I met Loren, an eighty-year-old gentleman who had white, wispy hair; an infectious smile; and the clearest blue eyes I had ever seen. Immediately as he spoke with us backstage, it was as though I—or all of us—had known Loren for years. He laughed easily and had a sense of peace and confidence about him that put everyone at ease. Loren asked if he could use me for part of his talk. I wasn't sure what that meant but somehow knew this was important and agreed.

I really don't remember what I spoke about that night, although it related to how men grow spiritually through dedication to spiritual disciplines. My memory was drowned out by Loren's talk that followed my own. I introduced Loren, and he stepped onto the stage, taking me by the arm firmly, yet affectionately, and saying to the men there—probably eight hundred or so—that he would use me as a way to show the Father's heart for sons. That's what he called the men in the audience, "sons."

He grasped me and kept me close, all the while explaining how the Father brings sons to himself and then draws them ever closer to his heart, his voice, and his presence. He never lets go but continues to hold us close, whispering to us to see the world as he does. He lets us experience his heart and unique call to us, so that we can share the same with others, calling more and more sons and daughters to himself.

There was much more that Loren spoke about. His message was beautiful and powerful. When Loren finished, there were hundreds of men weeping, reaching out afresh and anew to receive what Loren had spoken about—a father's heart. When we stepped off the stage, Loren turned to me, looked at me with a deep insight that seemed to penetrate to my soul, and said, "Jeff, I think the Lord has some work for us to do together."

I immediately responded, "Yes, I am all in." Loren hugged me, and we walked into the crowd of men, where he was asked to pray with people and elaborate further on what he had shared. I marveled at his smile and affection for each person he spoke with. I knew there was a new journey ahead. God had provided a friend I could look to as someone over me—a spiritual mentor.

While that aspect of the relationship was yet to unfold, at the same time I began to sense that the Lord was prompting me to reach out to guys I had known from the past who had been significant in my life as friends or mentors in my early years of growth. One by one, I sent texts and made phone calls, with just a simple hello—How are you?—Care to get coffee sometime?

And one by one the guys responded, slowly at first, but we found in each case that we were missing the same things in friendship—the camaraderie we had shared earlier in our days of fresh fire in the Lord Jesus Christ. Then something else began to happen. I met some new guys who were like minded, had the same heart for the Lord, and wanted to have a friend who would come alongside, encourage, challenge, pray with, and stick close as brothers. What was happening?

As I was asking the Lord to connect me with guys who would want to walk together with me, he was showing me something like small rivers that were now moving. The fresh water of God's presence I was seeking and finding was moving forward in small streams. As that happened, God began to enlarge the waters and others came along; guys began to call, asking for fellowship and encouragement. Waters were flowing.

Living Water

Remember John 4 and Jesus speaking to a Samaritan woman at Jacob's well? In verses 10 and 13 Jesus speaks of living water that he offers, water that wells up into eternal life. Jesus was referring to the Spirit of God moving in a person like living water, refreshing, invigorating, and life-giving. Because the Spirit of the living God is in us, we have living water that we can experience and offer to others. When we understand and walk with purpose, our eyes on building up others and encouraging those around us, there is true living water spilling outward from us because it is filling us and overflowing to those with whom we come into contact.

My experience tells me that far too often we do not understand and therefore do not walk in the fullness of the Spirit of God who resides in us. However, when we walk as servants of the living God, desiring to have him use us in the lives of those around us to build them up, to encourage them, and to disciple them (and sometimes to light a fire under them), the Spirit of God moves in us and from us and takes those living waters into other people's lives.

Let that sink in. Jesus says we have living water moving in us. What are you experiencing right now of the Holy Spirit's presence and power inside you? Do you sense living water surging within you? If your answer is yes, outstanding! Walk deeply in it and let it spill out to others! If you don't sense living water, there is a simple solution. Ask the Father.

Jesus said that, if we ask the Father, he will give us the Holy Spirit. The Holy Spirit indeed enters our lives upon salvation – the new birth in Christ. Yet Jesus still invites us to ask. Jesus spoke of this when he said, "If you, then, though you are evil, know how to give good gifts to your children, how much more will your Father in heaven give the Holy Spirit to those who ask him!" (Luke 11:13). And again Jesus said, "Ask and you will receive" (John 16:24). Remember, the fullness of the Spirit is for us, and we are in our turn to pour it out to refresh others. When we do so it not only benefits others, but we paradoxically receive a greater inflow of even more of the fullness. The gifts of God come *to* us to *flow through* us.

Perhaps the real reason for the lack of evangelistic and discipleship fervor in us is the lack of understanding and reception of the Holy Spirit's empowering ability in and through us. It could well be the case that teaching about discipleship is not the solution for spurring some people to become disciple-makers. It may be, in fact, that there is little or no life of the Spirit being realized and therefore propelling such a believer into the life of discipleship about which Jesus spoke in Matthew 28.

Some of you reading this may have tried many different ways to live in discipleship and to be a disciple-maker. Yet this ideal hasn't been realized in your life. I would consider at this point the possibility that you need a fresh filling of the Spirit of God to accomplish what Jesus spoke about when he said to the disciples, "Stay in Jerusalem until you receive the gift my father promised" (Luke 24:49 NCV). He was speaking of the Holy Spirit. And what did he say of the Spirit's work in those believers and all of us who would follow?

Jesus said, "You will *receive power* when the Holy Spirit comes on you; and you will be my witnesses in Jerusalem, and in all Judea and Samaria, and to the ends of the earth" (Acts 1:8, emphasis added). In other words, the Lord is saying that he will be in us and will cover us with power. It is not enough for any believer just to teach discipleship. You must be able to impart power to another believer through the Spirit of God who lives in you and flows through you like living water.

There have been so many times in my life (and I'm sure there will be more) when I did not sense the moving of the Spirit within me. At such points I like to take time to get alone before God and to seek him afresh and anew. Most often I will put on worship music, get quiet, and begin to worship the Lord. In that space I seek the heart of God. I ask him to break me and to move in me once again.

The key is to not stop seeking God through worship and prayer until you sense the living water of the Holy Spirit on the move within you. I don't know how you sense the Holy Spirit's stirring, but I most often know that he's on the move within me because tears well up and I sense his presence and can't keep from weeping. Each person who has an intimate relationship with God will receive and know the Holy Spirit's presence in some way that he makes real to them.

Dear brother and sister, I would invite you to take time in the presence of the Lord and to seek him anew until he comes and falls freshly upon you like a soft rainfall, touching your heart and bringing you to a place of loving repentance and brokenness with whatever he chooses to show you. Then you will sense the water moving in and through you . . . the freshness of the Spirit of God, who loves you and raises you up to see his face and to know his call on your life to reach others.

In Isaiah 6 this is exactly what happened to Isaiah, who was in his older years of ministry. After the king of Judah, his close friend, had passed away, he turned to the Lord in worship. He had a vision in which saw the holiness of God leading him to fresh repentance and a fresh call on his life. Here is that scene:

> In the year that King Uzziah died, I saw the Lord, high and exalted, seated on a throne; and the train of his robe filled the temple. Above him were seraphim, each with six wings: With two wings they covered their faces, with two they covered their feet, and with two they were flying. And they were calling to one another:
>
> > "Holy, holy, holy is the LORD Almighty;
> > the whole earth is full of his glory."
>
> At the sound of their voices the doorposts and thresholds shook and the temple was filled with smoke. "Woe to me!" I cried. "I am ruined! For I am a man of unclean lips, and I live among a people of unclean lips, and my eyes have seen the King, the LORD Almighty." Then one of the seraphim flew to me with a live coal in his hand, which he had taken with tongs from the altar. With it he touched my mouth and said, "See, this has touched your lips; your guilt is taken away and your sin atoned for." Then I heard the voice of the Lord saying, "Whom shall I send? And who will go for us?" And I said, "Here am I. Send me!" (Isaiah 6:1–8).

Through Isaiah's worship he experienced the pure waters of the holiness of God and received God's personal call in a fresh new way. It is vital to stay in a place of awe, where we daily meet with the Lord to receive new levels of his Word and presence to fill us, nurture us, and nourish us so that we may comfort, encourage, and nourish others.

Chapter 9

Reaching Out to Be a Disciple-Maker:
Rivers and Streams

A Lesson from the Landscape of Israel
There is a picture of Israel and its geographical landscape that reveals specific truths and opens up for me the greatest understanding of discipleship I have discovered in terms of reaching out to people. The picture is of the region of Israel that contains the Sea of Galilee, the Jordan River, and the Dead Sea.[6]

The Sea of Galilee, where Jesus spent so much of his ministry with his disciples, teams with life. It is fed by the Jordan River from the north and from underground springs. As water flows into the Sea of Galilee, it also flows out southward to the Dead Sea, which receives this fresh water via the Jordan River. But that's where it ends because the Dead Sea has no outlet. It doesn't share its waters anywhere else, so the Dead Sea water, which once had life—no longer does. As a body of water, the Dead Sea is just that—dead. The lesson here is quite clear. Even though fresh water flows in and fills and feeds and nourishes, unless it finds an outlet there will be no life.

This is a picture of our lives. The pure water of the Word of God and the Spirit of God flows into us through many streams and rivers. What are the streams and rivers flowing into our lives? Of course, the number one stream, spoken of by Jesus Himself, is the Holy Spirit who lives in us. You may consider this the underground spring in our lives, similar to the continuous underground springs pouring fresh water into the Sea of Galilee. There are other Holy Spirit streams, however, that also spring up into life: the Bible itself, worship, the teaching of pastors, the fellowship of friends, and many media and written sources bringing the flow of life-giving spiritual water into us.

There is so much potential Holy Spirit water flowing into our lives that it's too hard to quantify. However, if there is no outlet river or stream from ourselves to other people, then what flows in simply evaporates and is gone like a mist, and we end up like the Dead Sea . . .unsavory and lifeless in our faith and experience, either wondering why we are missing something or simply ignorant of what we lack, happily "living the dream" but missing God's plan and purpose for us.

Fortunately, God has a remedy for this! He provides many streams and rivers to flow out of our lives. God wants to show us what these rivers and streams are and where they lead. We do not have to pick up a shovel or use an excavator to carve out of the earth conduits to various places in order to experience life. All we need do is to recognize the rivers and streams that God has naturally made available through us.

For example, do you have a family or are you part of a family? There are natural tributaries running from you to family members. Are you employed? There are plenty of river and stream possibilities where you work. Are you involved in sports or some other activities in which you interact with people? There are many outlets for the waters that can flow from us to others through our leisure activities. By the way, God has designed particular rivers and streams to flow from us based on our personalities and giftings and on who we are as his children. He has tailor made those rivers and streams. All we have to do is notice where they are.

Many believers do not understand the impact and definitive stance of Matthew 28:19, Jesus's directive for us to "go and make disciples of all nations." This is not a suggestion but Jesus's very commission to every believer. Too many have bypassed that mandate by feeling good about attending a church service once a week and possibly even giving to a church or ministry.

Remember, however, that Jesus did not say, "Go into a church service once a week and hear the gospel," "Go join a serving team at your church," or "Go into all the world and tithe." He said, "Go and make disciples." There is really one command we need to center on, and Jesus is counting on our following through, on our reaching out to those others he bought and paid for with his blood and body. He loves people so much that he gave himself willingly; let's not forget that he was slaughtered; broken; and, according to the Scriptures, beaten beyond recognition.

The sin of every human being who has ever lived or ever will live was placed on him. He was then separated from his Father and gave himself to die to pay the price for you, for me, for everyone. This is the Good News that compels us in our turn to go into all the world and make disciples. This is his will and our calling. The kicker: he has provided the power, the giftings, and the rivers from our lives to get it done.

Okay, so maybe you're believing by now that you are called to be a disciple-maker, and you understand that there are streams and rivers flowing in your life that Jesus has prepared for you to use in connection to people around you. How are you to sense or identify who it is who stands in need of the effluence of living water from you? It's really quite simple—who is on your mind? Yep, that's it—who is on your mind and in your sights? That's a person who might be thirsty for a drink of the living water you possess. You can start a conversation, a quite natural and practical conversation, and see where it leads.

I'll give you an example from my own experience. John is the father of a boy I coach. He shows up at practices and has asked to help. It is easy to observe that there is a stream waiting to run between my life and his. So, where do we start? With a yes, from me, to allow him to help. From there it is simply sharing conversation—family, background, interests, etc.—and listening really well to his thoughts and conversation.

As a listener, my first motivation is to affirm whatever he chooses to talk about. I don't have to have experienced everything he has experienced or felt everything that he has felt, but I can affirm his experience as valid and important. That's what we want people to do for us—to affirm us. We all want acceptance, understanding, and belonging. Affirmation means that I agree that what a person has experienced is valid, whether or not I agree with the person's perspective on the situation.

So, when my new friend explains his experience with the military, I listen and may possibly ask a nonthreatening, clarifying question. "What branch were you in?" "What was your experience like?" Over time I continue to listen and welcome his input. When it seems to be an understandable next step,

I ask if he would like to get coffee sometime and talk further. I don't recall a time when I was turned down. By the time I ask, we have established rapport and a friendship that is already growing. This is not a project but a relationship. It's a friendship. God cares about people, and he is asking me to care. To take the time to listen, walk together, and talk together—that is caring.

Chapter 10

Learn How to Listen

Spiritual Hearing

One of the questions I get asked more than any other is "When you meet with someone in a discipleship relationship, what do you do? Where do you start, and then where do you go with it?"

There is a way to understand how to meet with a person one-on-one. There is a process I noticed early on in meeting with people who wanted to talk, learn, and grow. I call it LEEP.

In meeting with people over the years, I began to recognize a pattern God was showing me that became familiar. Its principles define how I operate most often when I meet with someone. This is just one pattern, and the Spirit of God works in an infinite number of ways; so, if it helps you, great. This is simply what has been effective for me and many others who have used it as a means to walk with someone in a friendship/discipleship relationship.

LEEP is an acronym for Listen, Encourage, Empower, Pursue.

Whenever we meet with someone, our first responsibility is to *listen*. Before we begin to meet with them, we need to ask God to allow us not only to hear them but also to hear his voice inside us concerning them. This puts us in a position of patient and relaxed listening. Our goal is not to tell anything about ourselves or to get lost on a tangent but to listen to what the person we are with is saying. At the same time, on the inside, we're trying to be sensitive to the Holy Spirit's abiding presence and what he may be indicating. The Holy Spirit quietly advises us with thoughts, ideas, and connections.

Sometimes a Scripture may come to mind. We will find that, over time, this is a beautiful combination of listening to the person we're with and also to the Spirit of God inside us. As we listen, we do not need to comment. We simply consider what's being said by the person we are with and the sensitivities the Spirit of God gives us. Yes, this takes practice. But we will find that God leads wonderfully when we listen carefully. While we listen, we search for something positive to build on. That leads to the next step.

The first E is for the word *encourage*. I mentioned earlier that what people need—and that includes you and me—is affirmation. Encouragement is a key that unlocks everything that follows. Our encouraging a person validates that they, and what they've experienced, are important.

When we listen to someone, we may note small statements signifying ideas and decisions of this person that are positive. We need to reiterate and encourage those ideas and decisions. When a person hears encouragement and validation, life and faith flow into them. When someone knows that we're not a threat but are in fact alongside to encourage and applaud particular things in their life, they begin to trust. Most importantly, wind begins to fill their sails, and they find hope.

In studying the etymology of the word *encourage*, we find that the root word, *courage*, has to do with "heart, spirit, and innermost feelings." The prefix *en* means to "put into." When we encourage someone, we are literally breathing courage, heart, and life into them. This type of encouragement allows for the next E, standing for *empower*.

To empower goes beyond encouragement, but encouragement is the basis. To empower means to give power and authority to someone. Empowerment happens when we have listened to the Spirit of God, and he has shown us something important from the Word of God to pass along. A Scripture or a truth to offer to this person has come to mind.

Power comes from the Word of God. Empowerment is not merely a solution; it's the ability to keep on, to endure with confidence that God gives sustaining ability to continue in any and every situation. Listening to the Holy Spirit is simply listening for the Word of God that applies to someone's situation.

This does not mean that we need to rush to offer a Scripture or to pray for a person. These steps may apply, but only after we've listened well and been able to encourage. Then, when it becomes obvious that the Word of God is applicable and powerful in a situation, we can offer it. The Word of God and prayer are means that bring to bear on the situation the power of God.

It may be that, after we have listened and encouraged, the person is seeking to understand how the Word of God can give them power in their situation. This individual may consider how the Word of God applies to their set of circumstances, but when this application and empowerment are affirmed the truth needs to become a declaration—something that is spoken. Usually, a promise from the Word of God needs to be spoken, so that not only does the person receive it but the devil hears it and has to stand down. I will go into detail about this in a chapter dealing with understanding spiritual warfare later in this book.

Quite often empowering someone means speaking a truth with or over them and having them repeat it out loud themselves. At times we may even have them write it down on a piece of paper, or they may write it as a note on their phone.

The *P* in LEEP means to *pursue*. This concept has a couple of ideas attached to it. The first: after encouraging the person we're talking with, we want to see them empowered to pursue the direction God has given. This is forward motion and is vital to taking a stance and taking steps on what God has shown. Pursuit might include pursuing the Word of God further, or it might call for an important conversation with another person. Pursuit may point to a time of worship and prayer and praise. In any of these instances, pursuit is what God shows that person to do in order to move forward. The second idea: to pursue also means that we continue to pursue this person as a friend and as a disciple we care about.

What I'm about to write next is going to seem like redundancy and possibly overkill, yet it cannot be overstated. Your time spent in the Word of God, to read, to study, and to continually pursue what the Lord is saying through that Word, is the rock-solid basis for this process I have just explained.

I pray that you will understand the importance of what I'm writing about now. While God has wired you personally for the people you connect with, you are most effective when you have a deep relationship with God through his Word. The more you study, the more the Lord will reveal to you, . . . and I have found that, whatever he reveals, we generally find an opportunity to use that day or very soon thereafter.

It is an amazing truth that, as we honor the Word of God, he honors the relationships and streams that flow from us into other people's lives. I've heard some refer to sharing the Word of God as having "a word in season." A word in season is just that: whatever season of life or situation someone is in, the Word of God that has been hiding inside you after you have stored it away will come to mind at the appropriate moment through the Holy Spirit's influence. You will hand that off to person after person, and God will use that in powerful ways.

Let me explain through an example. Some years ago, I was impressed to study the book of Psalms. It was interesting to learn about the five divisions of the Psalms and the various writers, and of course, the seasons of life and situations these authors were in when they wrote. So much of their journeys pertain to us and where we find ourselves at many times in our lives. One psalm that stood out was Psalm 84; I made a great connection with it because of the things I was walking through at that time.

The psalm starts beautifully as it reads, "My soul yearns, even faints, for the courts of the LORD; my heart and my flesh cry out for the living God"

What stood out to me then and still stands out to me now are four things, the first being that God recognizes that our hearts are on a pilgrimage with him; a pilgrimage means a journey of ups and downs with all kinds of possibilities. The second point is the word "Baka," which means a place of bitter weeping. In other words, while we are on our pilgrimage, the Lord knows we will go through times of bitter weeping, and these times are meaningful to him.

As I read this, I sensed his overwhelming compassion toward us. That leads to the third point, which is powerful. Our tears become a place of springs or pools of water. Those pools of water are springs that become life-giving. The life-giving element is what our hearts receive from the Lord and his compassion and what we in turn are able to offer to others, so that they can become pools of living, healing water for still others.

The fourth point has to do with the autumn rains. If you are agriculturally minded, you probably know that the preparation for the next growing season relies on the autumn rains that saturate the ground with at least 75 percent of what the soil will need for the next year's yield. God uses those tears we shed in sorrow to build up pools and springs that will enrich both ourselves and other people. To top that off, he sends his refreshing autumn rains that prepare the soil: our hearts and lives, as well as the hearts and lives of those around us.

This was my fresh understanding of Psalm 84. It has enriched me over and over through the years. However, I said I would show you how storing up the Word of God like this can be used as a "word in season" for someone else. Here is the connection.

Because of the richness of this psalm and its connection to my life, I have been able to refer to it several times when someone has been in pain or sorrow and needs to know that God is near and offers hope. Because this study in Psalm 84 is rich and meaningful to me, God uses it over and over to comfort, encourage, and strengthen people I meet with in discipleship. The Word of God stored up within us—the Word of God you store within you—the Lord will bring up at key times to enrich others, to give them hope, life, and the encouragement that they are not alone.

Whenever we invest our time in the Word of God, whenever we honor the Word of God by studying and yearning to know the Lord through his Word, he grows rich fruit in us that is nourishing for us personally but also grows a crop that other people will consume and enjoy time after time as the Word of God becomes a storehouse that feeds many. Those fresh pools of water that were once tears become the water of life for us and others.

Chapter 11

Streams, Rivers, and Transparent Waters

Have you ever watched a stream move along that was filled with sediment and dirt and was darkened because of harmful elements that were floating in it? Likewise, have you looked into a stream or river that ran clear and been able to see everything through it as if it were transparent glass? It is mesmerizing to gaze on the purity and clarity of swiftly moving, clear waters.

Which appeals to you more? If you had to, which would you dare to take a drink from? Of course, we would all answer, "The pure, clear stream." Yet our lives at points have been muddied, dirtied by poor decisions, habits, mistakes, and reactions to the ways we may have been treated. Are they unusable by God? Have the past issues made us unsuitable, muddied waters? Absolutely not. In fact, God can use all of it. And he does so very well. He takes those muddied waters of our lives and transforms them into clear streams that he is free to use when we share in a transparent manner.

I have found that the trials, tears, heartaches, and mistakes in our lives are often the connecting points in the streams and rivers of sharing life with another person. While I realize that we need to trust that anything personal we share will be guarded, it seems to me that many people may be overly cautious about concealing the trials and mistakes of their lives. Why do we have tests? So we can have a testimony. Why is life so often a mess? So we can have a message. A test becomes a testimony, and a mess becomes a message.

When spending time with someone in mentorship and discipleship, or just sharing friendship, as I have listened and sought the Lord about points that will make connections, quite often he has brought something to mind that is heartfelt or even heartbreaking that could possibly be shared. I do this carefully, yet I've learned to do it freely. My hardships, my pain, and my mistakes are quite often what someone else needs to hear to encourage them that they're not alone.

This is the element of transparency that allows someone to see into my life and realize that, not only has someone else faced trials and heartache, but they now have someone with them who understands and will empathize with where they are at and what they have experienced. When offered tenderly as a friend in careful conversation, such sharing can be a spring of life that allows people to get past what have been major roadblocks and on to the next steps toward eventual healing.

I will add that I usually let the friend know their conversation is safe with me. Unless they want any further involvement with others, and ask for it, their story goes no further. Also, my conversation includes letting the friend know I am along for the journey and that I am a friend who can be trusted for the road ahead.

What I am about to share is hard to write about, but I offer it as a way to be transparent with heartache. I believe many of you can relate. When I was just a year and a half old, my mother had a new baby, a brother, who was named Mark. I also have an older sister named Pam. My mother, soon after giving birth, lapsed into a coma. She was in what my father called a "visual coma," with her eyes open for the duration, which lasted two and a half years.

During that time my father was working during the day as an engineer at Michigan State University and then heading to the hospital after work. My sister and I were sent to my grandparents' farm in New Brunswick, Canada, where my dad had grown up. My brother Mark, being so young, was sent to live with an aunt and uncle not too far from my dad's house in Lansing.

Spending the better part of two years on that farm meant that it became my home as a young boy. I suppose I was too young to understand when my grandmother sat my sister and me down one day and said we were to return home to Michigan. She did not explain that my mother had passed away in the hospital but only that it was time to leave.

I was not quite four years old, and I didn't want to go—this was the family I knew. My grandmother tried to console me and told me that my sister and I would be okay and that I had a little brother waiting to meet us. When I heard about the brother, I was eager to meet him! Mark and I became fast friends and buddies; we did everything together over the years, from sports to the trouble we got into and, of course, everything we could think of to antagonize and annoy our sister. As they say, "boys will be boys!" Pam endured a lot of our shenanigans over the years but was a warm, comforting leader to me.

My dad remarried, and he and my stepmom over the years had five more kids. We were an energetic, crazy bunch. My brother Mark, though a year younger than me, got married first. I was the best man at his wedding. This was an amazing time in my life. A year later I proposed to my fiancée, Anne, and asked my brother Mark to be my best man. What a great exchange!

Anne and I were living in Houston, Texas, and were brand new elementary school teachers, enjoying life in the South. Anne had an apartment with a friend, and I lived with a retired couple from our church not far away. The wedding was to be in Michigan that summer. We made plans from across the country, and I collaborated with my brother, looking forward to the end of the school year and returning home for the wedding.

On Memorial Day that year, just weeks before the wedding, however, my dad called and asked me to sit down, wherever I was. My heart sank before knowing anything else. What was he going to tell me that required me to sit? He went on to explain that my brother and a friend had been at a northern Michigan lake cottage with friends for a celebration. He and a buddy had gone out on the lake in a canoe around midnight, and the canoe had capsized. It was found on the shore on the far side of the lake the next morning.

My brother Mark and his friend were nowhere to be found and were believed to have drowned. Because the temperature of the lake was very cold in the spring, the bodies surfaced after a couple of weeks. We buried my brother just twelve days before he was to be the best man at my wedding.

In Mark, I lost my brother, my best man, and my close friend. The weeks that followed were hollow, except for our wedding. My bride was beautiful, and our pastor, John, along with my best friend, Jeff Williams, gave deep and meaningful marriage messages. For the first time in my life, I felt the tangible presence of God as I looked at the space where my brother was supposed to be standing as my best man.

Incredibly, I experienced a combination of deep sadness and peace in that moment. I had a comfort beyond explanation, elevated by the innocent, pure beauty of my bride. I would be remiss not to mention that I lay awake in tears for many nights following, unable to sleep, wishing I had another chance to see my brother. I missed Mark more than words could ever describe.

I know tragedy. But I also know comfort. I know deep hurt . . . and deeper healing. If I were to go on, there would be, as with you and your life story, more to tell.

The Lord says in his Word, ". . . to comfort all who mourn, and provide for those who grieve in Zion—to bestow on them a crown of beauty instead of ashes, the oil of joy instead of mourning, and a garment of praise instead of a spirit of despair" (Isaiah 61:2, 3). He tells us that he "heals the brokenhearted and binds up their wounds" (Psalm 147:3) and adds that "in all things God works for the good of those who love God, who have been called according to his purposes" (Romans 8:28).

We know that, whatever events come into our lives, the Father in his love, tenderness, and mercy will comfort us and somehow, someday, use our brokenness and sorrow to build up someone else in their own time of need. These conduits, too, are streams and rivers. Transformed by the love and grace of Father God, they are crystal clear as they flow from our lives to others.

It is amazing how the Lord uses our pain. He is not callous or cavalier about what we endure; he himself suffered far more than we will ever know, so he knows how to take our scars and make of them character. He takes the pit and makes it a pasture, takes the tears of tragedy and makes them pools of healing—cool, cleansing waters.

Why was Jesus able to comfort and understand the leper, the prostitute who was broken, or the parent whose child was demonized? Because he himself suffered in his body. We have a faithful high priest who was tempted in every way as we are—yet was without sin (Hebrews 2:17). He understands. Likewise, we are broken at times, . . . and then we understand. What we have suffered, what we have endured, becomes the ministry we offer to others—a ministry of understanding and hope—just as the Lord has ministered healing and hope to us and will continue to do so all our life long.

We Minister Best as Broken Bread

When Jesus fed the five thousand in Matthew 14:13–21, he first broke the bread. He then handed the morsels to his disciples, who distributed them to the people. Notice particularly here that Jesus first broke the bread. It was not useful until it was broken in his hands. The miracle occurred when the disciples handed it out to the people to eat. Only then was it multiplied.

This picture offers a great connection to our lives. When we come to Jesus Christ and ask him to glorify his name by using our lives on behalf of others for discipleship and the winning of souls, our lives first become the bread that will be broken in his hands. *Broken in the Master's hands*, we are distributed and multiplied in miraculous ways.

In 2 Corinthians 1:3–7 the apostle Paul shares this concept. He writes,

Praise be to God and Father of our Lord Jesus Christ, the Father of compassion and the God of all comfort, who comforts us in all our troubles, so that we can comfort those in any trouble with the comfort we ourselves receive from God. For just as we share abundantly in the sufferings of Christ, so also our comfort abounds through Christ. If we are distressed, it is for your comfort and salvation; if we are comforted, it is for your comfort, which produces in you patient endurance of the same sufferings we suffer. And our hope for you is firm, because we know that just as you share in our sufferings, so also, you share in our comfort.

Whatever we suffer leads to our brokenness, like bread in the hands of Jesus, which in turn leads to our comfort from the Father and then to the comfort of other people. There are two promises here, one being that we will be comforted! The second is that our comfort will be shared with others. This leads to an incredible connection: in the beauty of transparency, fresh, pure water is offered to the one you walk with in discipleship and connects your heart to their heart, your life to their life.

Chapter 12

Spiritual Warfare

Yes, My Friends, There Is a Devil

In 1897 an eight-year-old girl named Virginia O'Hanlon wrote a letter to the *New York Sun*, wanting to know if there really is a Santa Claus. Frances Church, a veteran writer for the *Sun*, was tasked with responding to the young Miss O'Hanlon. Within the editorial response came the renowned clause, "Yes Virginia, there is a Santa Claus." The phrase led to the creation of a song and a movie and has been translated into more than seventy languages.[7]

In a parallel idea, I would state, "Yes, my friends, there is a devil. The devil and his demons do exist. Many of you reading this will already understand that Satan was once an angel named Lucifer but was cast from heaven because of the pride that was found in him. Ezekiel records God's words to Lucifer: "Your heart became proud on account of your beauty, and you corrupted your wisdom because of your splendor. So I threw you to the earth" (Ezekiel 28:17).

The book of Revelation tells us that the devil swept one third of the angels of heaven with him in his deceit. He and his minions have become known as fallen angels, and they have plagued humankind from the beginning. Satan is not equal to God, and he is not the antithesis of Jesus. Satan is a fallen angel. Jesus is the Son of Almighty God, being in very form God, himself part of the triune Godhead.

Luke records Jesus saying that he saw Satan fall like lightning from heaven, and Isaiah 14 and Ezekiel 28 clearly describe how Satan was initially created, prior to his fall. It is true that Satan does have limited power. Yet Jesus is the King of kings and the Lord of lords, and he has all authority in heaven and on earth and, ultimately, all power over all things. According to the Scriptures, Satan and his legions will fight against the Lord and his offspring, which is us, believers in the Lord Jesus Christ, until they are taken out of the way. But their time hasn't yet come.

In effect, there are battles being waged day after day against believers in the Lord Jesus Christ. These skirmishes are the very things that train us to use the authority of the Lord Jesus and the weapons God has given us to be always at our disposal—weapons that are effective one hundred percent of the time. It is vitally important for every believer to know what these weapons are and how to use them. Please do not be discouraged by this. As someone who has coached at the high school and college levels, I can tell you what I believe to be the Lord's intention for us: he wants us to be in training to understand the battle we are in and how to fight properly so we will win against the enemy and lead others into victory as well.

To understand the battle means to understand yourself first. At what particular point of vulnerability do the devil and his demons target you? I'll bet it's the same thing over and over. This is the enemy's strategy. He picks an area of your life and continually lays siege to it until he finds an opening, after which he looks for a foothold. He wants to control that area of your life, whether it's physical, mental, emotional, or spiritual.

Ever read the book *Screwtape Letters* by C. S. Lewis? If not, I would suggest that you get a copy. Lewis reveals the strategy of the enemy and his plans against believers in the Lord Jesus Christ, offering "advice" to a young demon being trained to attack believers. The book is entertaining and yet very eye-opening.

I in no way want to make out the devil and his legions to be bigger or stronger than they truly are or to make them too much of a focus of our time and mental energy. However, I do want to represent the teachings of Scripture to equip us to gain victory for ourselves and others.

Victory: First Personal—Then for Others

When I first started to learn about the enemy and how he operates, it was through the Scriptures and the teachings of a pastor who knew the enemy is real. He pointed me to the Scripture texts that show the ministry of Jesus and how he dealt with Satan one-on-one, as well as to the demons that plagued people until Jesus cast them out.

I was especially intrigued by Paul's admonitions and teaching about the unseen forces of darkness. He writes, "Finally, be strong in the Lord and in his mighty power. Put on the full armor of God, so that you can take your stand against the devil's schemes. For our struggle is not against flesh and blood, but against the rulers, against the authorities, against the powers of this dark world and against the spiritual forces of evil in the heavenly realms. Paul also enjoined his readers to "stand firm, then, and do not let yourselves be burdened again by a yoke of slavery" (Galatians 5:1).

How the Trap Gets Set

A great example of a foothold becoming bondage is found in Genesis 3:1–6 when the serpent spoke to Eve about the fruit of the tree of the knowledge of good and evil. Initially, Eve knew the fruit was not to be eaten. Through the serpent's cunning marketing of this evil device, however, he managed to entice Eve just to look at it—which she did. This kind of seduction, often subtle, is what we refer to as temptation.

With her eyes lingering on this fruit, her attitude jumped from knowing that partaking of it would be evil to believing that this action would be good and acceptable. This lingering look became a longing, and it changed her view from submission to God to curiosity and from curiosity to agreement with the serpent. For Eve this long, lingering look became a foothold, and at this point Satan knew he had her. Bondage came when she took the fruit and ate of it . . . and convinced Adam to do the same. These seemingly innocent actions led to bondage so serious that it enslaved both them and the rest of the human race through all of history.

This is how the enemy works still today. He tempts us to focus on something that does not correspond with the will or plan of God. When we perseverate over something sinful or begin to obsess over it, believing it to be what we want, that longing becomes a foothold.

As a wrestling coach for over forty years, I can tell you that a foothold is a firm grasp of one wrestler on the foot or ankle of another. This second athlete is caught in the grasp of the opposer, who then has a great advantage over his opponent and can move him purposefully where he wants to. This leads to bondage; you are caught, subdued, unable to get away.

What common attitudes or emotions can become footholds? Among them are unforgiveness, lust, anger, jealousy, shame, regret, fear, pride, loneliness, and control issues. There are others, but you get the picture. When we focus on or give in to any of these negatives, just as Eve focused on the fruit on that tree in the garden, we get caught in a foothold by the enemy. Temptation turns to sin as we consider something sinful to be something sweet. Unless we do some immediate confessing and repenting, that foothold will likely become an area of bondage in our lives. This happens when we consume that "fruit" mentally, emotionally, physically, or spiritually.

The Solution: The Word of God

How can this be remedied? First, with confession, repentance, and prayer. By the way, confession most often has the greatest lasting value when it is made to another person after confessing to the Lord. Having another person you trust pray over you is also very powerful.

Next, it is vital to recognize why you are succumbing to temptation. In the moment of temptation, there needs to be a heartfelt response based on Scripture. When Jesus went face-to-face with Satan in the wilderness, every time he was tempted he answered Satan with words of Scripture. Jesus's response was with the Word that alone could counter Satan's temptation. This is the model for us in building up our spiritual lives and our minds to withstand the attacks of the enemy.

Every type of enemy attack can be countered with the Word of God. Our training must include memorizing the Scriptures for use when we are under any kind of attack. This is also true as we help others who are under various kinds of attacks from the enemy. Our knowledge and wise use of the Word can help set brothers and sisters free from the bondage of the enemy.

Do you feel that there are roadblocks in your own life that have caused you to question God and the freedom of your salvation? Are there secret areas you have covered up in your life that you wish you could get control of and gain freedom over? Take a few minutes and ask the Lord to reveal to you what areas of your life need freedom. I find the most common to be unforgiveness and bitterness.

Reread the list of problematic attitudes on page 86 and ponder whether one or more of those might be your issue. These mindsets and others like them are the roots of all kinds of issues with sin, and wallowing in any of them can result in mental, emotional, physical, and spiritual problems. Never forget that *our mind is the battleground within which the enemy attacks.* Do you have control over the attitudes and thoughts in your mind? God wants to and can give you freedom and control over your thinking—a first step in gaining freedom and control over your life.

The best way to understand Satan's tactics and the way he affects your life is to read the Scriptures that explain the basic truths about the enemy. Ephesians

6 is a great place to start. The apostle Peter also gives a strong admonition to us by, stating: "Be alert and of sober mind. Your enemy the devil prowls around like a roaring lion looking for someone to devour. Resist him, standing firm in the faith, because you know that the family of believers throughout the world is undergoing the same kind of sufferings" (1 Peter 5:8, 9).

Two truths stand out in this passage by Peter. First, we all are being sought after by the enemy. Second, we can resist him because we are part of an army worldwide that is called the church, the body of believers. There are many identity-related Scriptures that I have included in a chapter titled "You Are a Disciple of Jesus—Heart, Mind, Body, Soul, and Spirit." I would encourage you to read that final chapter and let the truths sink in of how highly God favors and loves you and the amazing things he says about you!

Speak It Out Loud!

Whenever we consider a promise of God that is important to memorize, especially to counter the attacks of the enemy, *when we use that Scripture it needs to be spoken.*

There's an important truth here. When Jesus was in the wilderness being tempted by Satan, with each temptation he responded with the Word of God that he spoke audibly to the devil. The devil and his demons do not have the ability to read our thoughts. Therefore, a Scripture or a prayer that we state or pray internally is not something they can respond to.

However, when we speak the Word of God, they hear it and must respond to it. It is important to understand that, whenever a promise of God given to us in Scripture applies to our situation, we need to declare it out loud. That is why the Word of God says, "Let the redeemed of the LORD tell their story" (Psalm 107:2). This is also why Jesus spoke to demonic forces. If you want further proof, just reflect on what Paul wrote to the Roman church about our salvation: "For it is with your heart that you believe and are justified, and it is *with your mouth that you profess your faith* and are saved" (Romans 10:10, emphasis added). Jesus said that, if we *confess* him before men, he will confess us before the Father. Confession needs to be spoken. This is a great spiritual truth and discipline to put into practice.

The Word of God implores us to read, study, meditate on, and store it in our hearts. When we make this our practice and really understand why we *need* that Word buried deep within us, it will speak *to* us, especially when we are embroiled in a battle of temptation or discouragement. The Word of God will come to mind at those points, and we will be empowered to use it as the sword it is, cutting to pieces lies, temptations, and despair.

Let me give you an example. When I was teaching middle school, I had five one-hour classes each day of English/language arts. That entailed dealing with nearly 140 students, not including the others who would stop by, the teachers, the staff, and the little rascals who insisted on being disciplinary problems. Many days there were interruptions and problems that occurred. After all, these were adolescents, with all of the adolescent angst and emotions erupting daily.

There have been times when I felt overwhelmed and overloaded and needed to get centered in terms of my perspective and actions as a true disciple of Christ in the classroom. On days like these, in between classes, I would walk to a staff bathroom, close the door, and speak the Word of God to myself. I would state biblical promises and scriptural truths to myself, like this:

"Henderson, you are a blood-bought child of God. Jesus Christ hung on a cross with nails through his hands and feet, bleeding out, just for you. You've been given the Holy Spirit of God, and you have an assignment from God himself. You are an evangelist and a shepherd to these kids. Satan has no hold on you, and he definitely can't defeat you. The Holy Spirit lives in you and is flowing out of you. His Word is your shield and sword. Where you stand is holy ground, and you can't be defeated, because you belong to the King of kings and the Lord of lords! Now go back into the classroom filled with the presence and Spirit of God and teach those kids; show them you love them and that Jesus Christ is calling to them through that love flowing through you!"

Freshly fired up from the truth of the Word of God, I would walk back into the classroom rejuvenated and encouraged, with the Word of God leaping in my chest. The day would be turned around by my speaking the truth of the Word of God to myself. If you have never done this, I would encourage you to speak these truths over yourself out loud and let the Spirit of God impact your mind, spirit, soul, and body. How often do you do this? That's an excellent question. You do this as often as you need to, to keep the edge of the sword, which is the Word of God, moving in you and through you to others.

Declaring the Word of God over Others

Several years ago, I had a precious, brilliant girl in my classroom, who was unfortunately plagued with anxiety. During that year we talked about and prayed over this, and she learned to trust the Word of God in tumultuous times of panic and fear. Although she moved on from my classroom to higher grades, over the next couple of years her anxiety grew worse, to the point of her experiencing panic attacks that would cause her to run, crying, down the hallway until she found my classroom.

I would take a break and talk to her in the hallway or in the nearby teachers' lounge. I would speak to her about God's perspective of her. I would speak over her that she is a precious daughter of the Most High God, who had created her wonderfully and calls her his own, making available to her hope and a bright future. Nothing negative in her past would negate God's plan for her, either then or in the future.

I would proclaim to her that God's love was in her and around her even in times of darkness and that he would be there with her and bring her out into his light. I would speak peace over her in the name of Jesus Christ. I prayed that she would sense and know that Jesus himself was holding her close through every fear. I would look at her and proclaim to her that God had set her free. I would speak to her about God's love as a Father for her and assure her that no weapon formed against her could ever prosper, because this was her inheritance in the Lord.

Gradually I would sense her breathing slowing down, and she would calm down and begin to repeat bits of what I was proclaiming to her. As she did, God's peace would calm her heart and mind, and she would know she would be okay. God had breakthroughs for her that would take time to fully emerge, but the Word of God declared over her and in her hearing would bring about more immediate breakthroughs and hope in her life in her moments of desperation. As a high school student, she started attending our church, even though she was the only one in her family who did so. She began to grow and serve and is an amazing young adult today who knows how to face her giants.

This is a practical example of declaring the Word of God over someone, but only one of dozens I could share with you. Over the years I've had parents and other teachers send me their kids who were plagued by anxiety, fear, depression, and other debilitating issues. Sometimes the situation required conversation, but always it ended with prayer and a declaration of the power of God's Word.

If there's something of the utmost importance I can get across to you right now, I want you to understand this: "Sharper than any double-edged sword, [the Word of God] penetrates even to dividing soul and spirit, joint and marrow; it judges the thoughts in the intentions of the heart" (Hebrews 4:12). The

Word of God was spoken, and worlds were birthed. The Word of God was spoken over dead bodies, and they became alive—think especially of the Son of God on the third day!

The Word of God is spoken by us, and God honors his Word. We receive our identity through what the Word of God says about us and who God is as a Father to us. I want you to understand how powerful and effective the Word of God is, not only for battling the enemy but in affirming who we are and whom we belong to! If you understand and believe that God is a merciful, loving Father to you, this truth alone will defeat many of the lies of the enemy in your life. You will learn to use the Word declared over the lives of others to see them set free to grow in his love and grace.

While the Word of God is exciting to see spoken over others to their benefit, I want to caution you to tread carefully. When you are talking with someone you are in a discipleship relationship with and sense a scriptural truth that can apply to that person or even be spoken to them or over them, it must be applicable, and the Holy Spirit must be the one leading.

Declaring the Word of God is not simply a nice idea or a kind gesture to offer. It is, after all, the very Word of God, led by the Spirit of God, to be carefully offered to someone else. My rule of thumb is this: if there is any question in my mind about whether or not to share a verse, I do not share or declare anything without first sensing the truth not only coming from the Word of God but also being applied by the Holy Spirit's leadership. I do not dare share anything that could be wrongly stated or misinterpreted or miss the mark. Having been too eager at times in my earlier days, I want to caution you not to be led by adrenaline but by the Spirit of God.

What everyone needs most when embroiled in a battle with the enemy is a friend to come alongside to hold a sword with them and to help them through.

Paul's Admonition to All Disciples in the Lord Jesus Christ

Many pastors, teachers, theologians, and authors have spent more than adequate time on the importance of the armor of God, as explained in Ephesians 6:10–19. Yet every time I consider the truth about who it is I belong to, the battle that is being waged, and the significance of how I need to prepare, I praise God for the clarity and encouragement I find in this portion of Scripture.

Let's get a firm grip on this section and delve into it to receive more truth and preparedness. Paul begins in Ephesians 6:10 with the simple word rendered in English as "Finally." This gives us the understanding that, of all the things he has written, he wants to impart last what is of the highest priority. We know that we remember best what is stated last. Paul's words, to follow, build to a crescendo in this victorious ending passage:

> *Finally, be strong in the Lord and in his mighty power. Put on the full armor of God, so that you can take your stand against the devil's schemes. For our struggle is not against flesh and blood, but against the rulers, against the authorities, against the powers of this dark world and against the spiritual forces of evil in the heavenly realms. Therefore put on the full armor of God, so that when the day of evil comes, you may be able to stand your ground, and after you have done everything, to stand. Stand firm then, with the belt of truth buckled around your waist, with the breastplate of righteousness in place, and with your feet fitted with the readiness that comes from the gospel of peace. In addition to all this, take up the shield of faith, with which you can extinguish all the flaming arrows of the evil one. Take the helmet of salvation and the sword of the spirit, which is the word of God. And pray in the spirit on all occasions with all kinds of prayers and requests. With this in mind, be alert and always keep on praying for all the Lord's people.*

Why is this section of Scripture so important for us to understand? So that we will know how to teach those we disciple that we as Christ's followers do battle every day. This is the norm and the expected Christian life. Even as we live to follow Jesus Christ, all the while the enemy plots and attacks.

As a wrestling coach I prepared my athletes mentally, physically, and emotionally. The training was daily, and I studied my athletes, looking to encourage and challenge them to learn and compete at the highest level possible. Each athlete would face tremendous opponents throughout the season, again and again. So, we trained over and over, practicing, looking at different scenarios, and becoming as prepared as possible.

Many of you know this routine and the tough training schedule required for many activities in your life. *Brothers and sisters, keep training!* And train others well. Our training and what we hand off to those we disciple will help them grow and meet the challenges of the Christian life head on. Let's face it, we are in a war. Don't be surprised at this, and remind the ones you disciple that this is the lay of the land. Everyone will be challenged. This is the way we grow best.

Check out this scenario from Judges 3. Joshua had passed on, and Israel was now headed by a variety of judges. At that time the tribes were supposed to be settled into the territories of Canaan, but they had not rooted out all of the ungodly nations from their lands. This is what the Lord said about that issue: "These are the nations the LORD left to test all those Israelites who had not experienced any of the wars in Canaan (he did this only to teach warfare to the descendants of the Israelites who had not had previous battle experience)" (Judges 3:1, 2).

Incredible. God wanted to make sure that this generation, the third out of Egypt, knew how to do battle. He set them up to be trained for battles. Notice that, right out of the gates in the New Testament, Jesus did the same with his disciples. They followed Jesus, and after his first major teachings, he led them to get into a boat. (Matthew 8:23-27) Following his direction, they immediately were thrown into a storm that could have ended their lives. They were terrified.

Wait, God . . . I came into this faith thing to be *safe* . . . or so I thought.

No, dear heart, you came into this faith thing to follow Jesus Christ, who is the host of the armies of heaven. First John 3:8 states, "The reason the Son of God appeared was to destroy the devil's work." Wow. Double wow. And we get to follow in his footsteps.

Christianity, the real kind, is *hard*. But it is also *good*. To be trained to win and to train others to win—what better assignment could there be?

You are a disciple-maker of those God brings to you to build up and raise up to follow him. My friend in discipleship, keep training. Through your continued faithful training you will stay sharp. The devil and his forces are always looking for an inroad, so train hard and train with those you disciple. Let them walk with you as you show them what training looks and feels like—show them the example of a person who is grounded in the Word of God, yet vulnerable. A disciple who leads—and yet follows closely the feet of the Master. A friend who, like Jesus, is faithful and can be counted on at a moment's notice.

Without question, spiritual warfare necessitates walking together, fighting the enemy together, engaging in battle together, and struggling together. There are no one-person armies. Be assured that your friends in the faith will love to walk with you, as you will learn to love to walk with them.

Chapter 13

Breakthrough: How to Lead in Discipleship with Endurance

Roadblocks. Wilderness periods. Winter-like seasons. Slow or no growth. All of these are common to every disciple of Jesus Christ.

In discipleship, one of the things I hear from every person at one time or another is that there is something in the way. A roadblock, a dry season, not feeling the presence of the Lord, getting nothing from the Word of God, and similar statements. I don't think I have ever met a believer in the Lord Jesus Christ who has denied experiencing one of these dilemmas.

Having just looked at spiritual warfare, the next thing to consider is whether there is a spiritual problem to be dealt with. If there is no obvious impediment, such as bitterness, unforgiveness, or another sin issue, quite often the Lord wants the person in this space to press in and to press on.

If the person you are walking with in discipleship truly wants to grow, and they experience a dilemma such as I am describing, it is time for them to dig in regardless of the landscape or environment. They need to continue to do the things that cause growth and nearness to the Lord, even without "feeling" anything. The farmer continues to water and weed the fields even though no sprouts are showing. At the right time all the measures taken will result in growth. There will be a breakthrough.

And just as a shoot breaks through the ground, so will each person who persists in seeking the Lord. When it's dry, seek water, more of the Word of God. When there is no fruit to be seen, continue to tend the tree, using the living Word of God and seeking sunlight—that is, the Spirit of God. The continuation of those things that seem to be routine disciplines are the elements that will prepare you for real growth at just the right time.

A lesson from nature. When a new lawn is planted and tended carefully with fertilizer and seed, the seed needs water almost constantly. However, there is a point at which a new shoot needs to experience "tension." If watering is withheld for just the right length of time, the tension from the lack of water will cause the roots to go deeper, giving the blades a better, stronger, and more enduring foundation in the earth. This truth of nature is a close analogy to what we can learn when we or those we disciple experience a "dry time," a "wilderness season." The tension of waiting isn't meant to kill us or to obliterate our faith; it is meant to allow us to grow deeper, seek longer, and let the Lord strengthen and elongate our roots of faith and trust.

Sometimes as we walk with the Lord we get the subtle idea that we are mature believers and hence fail to understand why the dry times and wilderness seasons occur. We will experience these instances all our lives long. In answer to this, the prophet Hosea urges his readers to "break up your unplowed ground; for it is time to seek the LORD, until he comes and showers his righteousness on you" (Hosea 10:12).

Notice what the Lord says to do with this dry ground of our spiritual lives. First, dig a plow blade into it. Pray. Read the Word. Confess what you know to be sin in your life. Confess to others where you are at. Listen to worship music and, most importantly, *worship*. Become thankful for who the Lord is, what he has done, and all that you have, including the people in your life. Thank him for your trials, as well. Psalm 100 reveals this truth: we "enter his gates with thanksgiving and his courts with praise." If you want to experience the presence of the Lord, continue to offer him thanks. Continue to bring him worship.

One of the greatest breakthroughs I have ever experienced came through my spiritual momma. We call her "Granny." Granny and her husband, Papaw, have poured meaningful discipleship into my wife and me for years. There was a time in my life when I was experiencing exhaustion, discouragement, and depression. I was in a dry period and grieving. I called Granny on the phone and poured out my heart to her, explaining all that I was going through. Granny very wisely told me, "Jeff, I think you should take that grief, that heartache, that depression and your tears, and offer them as a sacrifice to the Lord."

I hadn't realized I could do that or that the Father would receive such as an offering. But he does. And he did. I offered my tears, my heartache, and my sorrow, and he received and accepted them. He received and accepted *me*. The depth of what God accomplished through that offering brought hope and freedom to me. He receives and accepts us in every condition we are in, during any type of season or situation.

Dear friend, offer your heart to him in its dryness; in the wilderness; in fear, depression, darkness, or sorrow; and when you are grieving. He will receive you and accept your offering of brokenness. He loves you. I thank God for Granny and Papaw. Every one of us needs someone like them in our lives. I hope that you become a Granny or Papaw to others.

It is a quiet, immutable truth in God's economy that if you keep sowing you *will* reap. Hosea also wrote, "Sow righteousness for yourselves, reap the fruit of unfailing love" (Hosea 10:12). He writes this just before he directs, "break up your unplowed ground." What precedes the breaking up is the continuation of sowing, doing righteous things, doing good, serving, seeking the Lord, and planting. As you continue to press in, especially when you are not "feeling it," God will put his hand on the blade of the plow and take his truths deeper into your heart. New sprouts will break the ground, new springs will bubble to the surface, and new rains will nurture the ground. Breakthrough *will* happen!

When talking with a friend who is experiencing dryness and feels alone, I know that I need to encourage them to continue on, to reassure them that the very things that were once life giving for them will bear life again, but in new and fresh ways. In Revelation 2:4–5 Jesus explains to the Ephesian Christians, "You have forsaken the love you had at first. Consider how far you have fallen! Repent and do the things you did *at first*" (emphasis added).

What did you do when you first met Jesus? I'll bet you were enamored by the freedom, the freshness of the Word of God, the joy and discovery in fellowship with other believers, and the excitement of sharing your faith! Do, again, what you did at first. Some will protest, "But I don't *feel* it . . ." Remind them that this is the kingdom of God and that in his kingdom there are reversals of human logic. You give and then you receive. You serve rather than being served. You are willing to sacrifice rather than to live a selfish life. For the believer, faith trumps feelings. You do the things you did at first out of faith, not feelings, knowing that God will bring the feelings later. Do the things you did at first—and trust that the Lord will honor your faithful obedience.

By the way, when I counsel those who are struggling in their marriage, quite often I will ask what their spouse was like when they met and what they loved about each other. I want to take them back to that "first love." What was it like? What was the fresh relationship like, and how did they celebrate it? I often encourage a husband or wife to release whatever barriers they are holding on to and return to their first love by doing the things they did at first. Remember, what we sow, we reap. Sow "first love" actions from the heart—and reap "first love" relationship again.

It is vital to remind and encourage those we mentor and disciple to continue on, to keep doing the things they did at first—and maybe try a new way of doing those things. Instead of sitting in the same old chair and reading the same old underlined passages, get up and take a walk and listen to the Word of God being spoken audibly. Most Bible apps offer that feature. Break religious traditions and routines by changing things up. For example, speak the Word of God out loud instead of just reading it silently.

Here is a game changer for me: singing the words of worship songs as I listen. My voice poured out in unison with the singer's awakens the soul and brings Spirit-filled air into my lungs! Prayer-walking: it is fresh and invigorating. The movement makes a difference in the activity. Praying during a workout, such as on a treadmill, builds faith while building endurance. Listening to a pastor or teacher during a workout or while engaged in daily tasks, such as doing the laundry, mowing the lawn, or making a meal, brings joy and clarity even to mundane tasks.

Calling a friend to meet and pray with is a great change-up. Making a new and creative journal for prayer and notes is a great idea for those who like to add detail and color to their journaling. Making a podcast or video about a favorite verse or book of the Bible or about a truth that is valuable is a creative opportunity for some.

Probably one of the most overlooked ways to break through dryness and wilderness seasons is to find some way to serve. This takes the eyes off a specific situation that might be holding us down and moves us in an outward and forward direction toward someone who needs help. What kind of service should you offer? A listening ear, a meal, a visit, a phone call, a text, a dinner.

If you are married, finding a place to serve together is a great move. Parents can (and should) take their kids on service opportunities. Every neighborhood has someone in need of lawn work, painting, or home repair or who just might appreciate some homemade cookies to cheer them up. These are ways to "break up unplowed ground" by sowing righteousness . . . and then reaping the fruit of unfailing love! Breakthrough *will* happen.

Chapter 14

The Disciple as a Servant

The importance of serving is monumental for the follower of Christ, and the desire to serve the Lord by serving others is the heart of discipleship. I want to outline three vital aspects of our lives that we are equipped to use in service to the Lord and to the people around us.

Teaching Discipleship: Serving with Time, Talent, and Treasure

One of the key aspects of discipleship that is important to impart to those we disciple is the understanding of what we have available to give and serve. Everyone has a certain amount of time, a variety of talents, and an amount of treasure in the form of what we call money. When teaching a young disciple about the importance of serving, these three areas are essential to know and understand.

God is the picture of giving. In terms of time, it is essential to bear in mind that he created us for relationships and longs to spend time with us. As James puts it, "He jealously longs for the spirit he has caused to dwell in us" (James 4:5). When it comes to talent, God passes along aspects of his creative genius in a myriad of ways to us, his image-bearers. He lifted mountains from the earth and created landscapes, sunrises, and sunsets that mesmerize even the greatest of artists. He uses creativity to access the path of someone's heart to discover Jesus Christ. He turns events around in ways that we could never script and that are precise and stunning to consider.

In like manner God lavishes on us his time, talent, and treasure, the wealth of heaven: his own dear Son as a price beyond comprehension for our redemption and to pay for the sin of humanity. What God offers to us he has fitted us with: not only time and talent but also treasure. What we do to offer these gifts to people around us is one of the main aspects of discipleship. in effect, the creative genius of God flows through us to serve people around us in creative and beautiful ways! Let's consider each of these giftings in more depth.

Time. We all have 24 hours a day, 168 hours a week, 672 hours a month, and 8,064 hours a year. The average life expectancy is now 77.28 years. This means that we can expect the possibility of 623,185.92 hours in a lifetime. We have been given many gifts and natural skills we can develop that can be used to work and to serve, to make a difference in the world around us. All of these giftings can be utilized within the framework of the time we have been given.

The time we have to offer others is truly a gift. To love, mentor, disciple, and care is life giving. When someone commits their time to another with no price attached, the receiver understands that a precious and powerful exchange has taken place. Giving of your time activates both the natural and the supernatural. In the natural world, fellowship unites hearts and lives. It offers hope. Someone who is offered your time receives the vital message that they are valued. That statement, that reality, can change a life.

In the supernatural realm, God moves *because* you are sacrificing your time to make someone else a priority. Sacrifice gets God's attention because that is the economy he lives in and presides over. He smiles on your offer of sacrifice. When David prophesied about Jesus, he wrote, "Sacrifice and offering you did not desire, but a body you prepared for me" (Hebrews 10:5, quoting from Psalm 40).

That's what we all have—a body to be used in his service. Each of us as a disciple can offer our lives—our bodies, as it were—as a sacrifice of time. As a father, I can tell you that, during many, many times when life was hard for my kids to understand, their comfort and security came in the form of a body: my own or my wife's; it was all about our taking the time, bodily and tangibly, to *be* with them, in the tough moments. That is true with anyone we disciple. Our presence will always signify security and comfort, even when there is no apparent answer to the trial through which they are suffering.

Talent. What are you good at? Maybe several things. You have natural abilities and skills you have acquired, along with spiritual gifts. All of these are tools you can use to serve the Lord by serving others. In John 13, as one of his last messages to his disciples, Jesus takes off his outer garment and wraps a towel around his waist. Taking off his garment is an extreme act of humility for the Son of God, yet he shows what we must do to serve well: we must humble ourselves, "take off" the outer garment of our pride, that garment that perhaps showcases our position, and serve from the heart.

The key here is to *take off* everything that hinders and holds us back. To serve as Jesus did is the first act of obedience in serving with our talent. That service must be unconditional, not based on the person or anything we might expect to receive in return. When Jesus served his disciples, he knew that one would deny him and another betray him to his death. Those heartbreaking events happened within hours after Jesus had washed their feet, fed them, taught them, and loved them better than anyone else ever had.

Serving with your talent is once again noticing where streams and rivers are possible. If you have an ability and are needed, step into that water and let the Lord lead you to make a connection that is important for someone. God will give you insight and lead you as you offer your abilities. One of the great blessings of serving is to serve with an "open hand." This means that you are giving of your time and offering your hands and abilities freely. In this day and age it seems as though many people give so they can get something in return. The freshness of offering your talents freely will invite someone else to have an attitude of thanksgiving and wonder. This can open a door that otherwise would remain closed.

If you can work on a car, that is a great gift to offer. If you can work on electronics, remodel, repair, do hair and nails, give music lessons, tutor, offer childcare, or open up time to write letters to prisoners, all of these and more are ways to offer your talents.

If you are wondering where to begin, ask the Lord; then look around you for where you can plug in. God will open a door and create a stream. Follow it and watch the Lord build another's life and faith through the gift of your talents!

Treasure. The giving of our finances is possibly one of the most difficult areas to understand and do wisely. I am not going to take time here to discuss the theology of tithing and free will giving. My point of emphasis is simply to give in response to a need that you can help with, or as a blessing to someone.

Discerning when and where to give your money can involve quite a learning curve. One consideration is whether a financial gift or buying something for someone else will be beneficial in your discipleship. What I can offer is to share my experience and what I have learned. I have given financially to those who have definite needs. I rarely give anyone cash, preferring to purchase for them something specifically needed. An offer to help in this way has quite often served to make clear not only what the need is but also whether the person asking truly has a need.

The idea behind giving your time, talent, and treasure is to serve. It is absolutely necessary and part of the fabric of a true disciple to discover how and where to serve. When Jesus spoke about the sheep and the goats in Matthew 25, he cited six specific ways to serve. This is not an exhaustive list but does offer a variety of ways to use time, talents, and treasure in service to others. Jesus spoke about feeding those who are hungry and thirsty, offering shelter to a stranger, clothing those in need, comforting the sick, and visiting those in prison. All of these require time, talent, and our personal treasure.

It is too common in our church culture to believe that just attending church and putting something in the offering is all that is necessary and expected. However, if we offer no true service from the heart toward others, we are deceived about the call of discipleship and in danger of becoming a Dead Sea, with blessings pouring in but nothing flowing out.

When working with those we disciple, it is important to devote much time to discerning when and how we can effectively serve. I have found that this is not often quickly discovered.

The Lord wants us to go on a journey of discovery. To find where we can most effectively serve really has everything to do with the spiritual gifts we have received and the natural skills and abilities we possess. If someone is unsure of their spiritual gifting, it's a good idea for them to read 1 Corinthians 12, along with Ephesians 4 and Romans 12:7–9, all of which explain spiritual gifts.

The next step is to identify the particular gifts a person has. There are many online tools for exploring your spiritual gifts. Keep in mind, however, that it is not enough just to know your gifts. You have to know your temperament as well. This determination will help you to recognize practical dynamics, like whether you like to lead or would rather come alongside to support. You may be either introverted or extroverted, which will have something to do with where and how you feel comfortable serving. Someone who is gifted with teaching may have the temperament for teaching adults but may flounder in a class of three-year-olds! There are temperament surveys you can find online to help you define just where you fall on the scale.

Jesus declared that he didn't come to be served but to serve and to give his life as a ransom for many (Matthew 20:28). Discipleship must have the element of serving if it is to be complete. We are at a point in our culture when the *self* is at the forefront of most media campaigns and advertising. There are many "self-help" messages and self-centered initiatives that keep people pursuing their ideal image, identity, power, and purpose, all outside of a biblical, Christ-centered belief system. When Christ comes first, serving is both a natural step and a healthy pursuit. We find identity through serving.

Sometimes we wonder why those we walk with in discipleship seem to gain little or no traction. Often the issue is that they have their eyes on themselves: what suits them, fits their likes and dislikes, and feels right. Learning to follow Jesus Christ as a disciple is a process of allowing the Spirit of God to walk with us and learning to follow his leading.

Early in my walk with Christ, I responded to what I wanted to do, went where I wanted to go, and made most decisions without prayer and consideration of what the Lord wanted. I did basically what my mind and body wanted to do. The growth in discipleship that took place in my life through friends, mentors, and the Word of God, however, showed me a model of how to follow the Spirit and seek his will for my life. To be truthful, the Lord still has to point out times and places where I need to discern between what I want and what the Lord wants me to see and understand.

The key here is to learn how to follow the leadership of the Spirit of the Lord.

The Litmus Tests of Serving: A Heart for People

Jesus didn't mess around with this test of serving. Check out Matthew 25 and brace yourself—the reflection might hurt. In Matthew 25 Jesus teaches about himself sitting on his throne in heaven and separating people one from another as a shepherd separates sheep from goats. The sheep he places on his right—a place of honor and acceptance—while the goats he removes and places on his left—a place of dishonor and rejection.

To those on his right, he will say, "Come, you who are blessed by my father; take your inheritance, the kingdom prepared for you since the creation of the world. For I was hungry and you gave me something to eat, I was thirsty and you gave me something to drink, I was a stranger and you invited me in, I needed clothes and you clothed me, I was sick and you looked after me, I was in prison and you came to visit me" (Matthew 25:34–36).

There it is—six things that would indicate a heart that is yielded to God. *The true tests have to do with the heart.* God can send you anywhere and ask you anything, and because you love him you will follow. The issue isn't so much the six specific ways to serve Jesus cited here. It is about truly following where the Lord leads, noticing what is needed, and responding to what God prompts you to do.

It is interesting that, when you read further in Matthew 25, the righteous ones Jesus refers to as being welcomed into his Father's glory are surprised at their acceptance. You see, they were simply doing what they were led to do because they saw a need; they had Jesus's heart. So, their service wasn't religiously motivated or a "must do." They were driven by a heart to care about what Jesus and the Father care about—people. Have you ever prayed that famous prayer, "Lord, break my heart with the things that break the heart of God?"

I have a good friend who was an avid church attendee. He showed up every Sunday, had his family with him, gave financially, and made certain his kids participated in the youth group. He and his wife attended a small group as well. A few years ago we were talking together about what it means to follow the Lord, and he tried to justify his relationship with the Lord by citing his church attendance. Yet he seemed to be looking for my affirmation of his concept of obedience—church attendance and the like.

I suggested we look at Matthew 25 and read through it together. When we had finished, I asked him, "Have you ever prepared a meal for someone outside your family who was needy and couldn't pay you back?" His answer was a slow, "No, not outside of my family or reunions or church gatherings." I went on. "Have you ever seen somebody thirsty during a hard day's work and just stopped and handed them a bottle of water and thanked them, asking if there was anything else you could do?" His answer was a definite "Nope."

I proceeded, "Have you ever opened up your home to somebody who needed a place to stay for a while?" His quick response was in the negative. I continued, "Have you ever bought new clothes for someone who couldn't afford them, outside of your family and your kids?" His reply, rather slowly stated, was no. I then asked, "Have you ever gone to the hospital to visit somebody outside your immediate or extended family who was sick and spent time with them? This time his answer was clear, "No, the only time I've been to the hospital to visit someone was when my kids were born."

Finally I asked, already quite certain of the answer, "Have you ever gone to a jail or prison to visit someone and encourage them?" He replied, "No, I've never gone to a prison or even considered doing so." By that point my friend's face had gone somewhat pale. No kidding—a deepening conviction was evident all over him. I looked at him and asked, "Do you realize that you've never done anything Jesus describes in these verses?" He responded in a measured tone, "I guess . . . I've never really considered these as important. I've spent my life taking my family to church and doing the things most Christians do."

Again, I have to emphasize that it isn't the works we do that validate our walk as disciples; rather, it is a heart turned toward God, so that no matter what he shows us to do, no matter how he shows us to serve, we are willing to do so because we love him and want to have mercy and compassion on those around us. Every person was created by God to know him and have a relationship with him, and the best way for people to come to that realization is by our serving them from the heart, as Jesus did.

I don't think my friend truly knew what his life's mission was. He thought it was simply about attending church and giving financially, being there and being somewhat involved. If that is all there is to our service, it sounds quite boring to me. I like the adventure of mission both inside and outside the walls of the church—of making disciples.

I do have to add as an addendum that the friend I mentioned has gone on to impact the lives of many people, something I have witnessed again and again as he has reached out in ways that are awe inspiring. Growth (both our own and that of others) is natural when serving from the heart is our gold standard.

Chapter 15

Learning to Listen to the Leading of the Holy Spirit and Helping Those You Disciple to Hear Him as Well

When we read the book of Acts, it is very apparent that the Old Testament Scriptures and those things Jesus had said to his disciples came to mind, through the Holy Spirit, as his apostles and other disciples led people to Jesus Christ and into discipleship. Jesus said in John 10, "My sheep hear my voice." If you are going to know the will of God, you will have to know how the Holy Spirit speaks to us and learn to perceive how he nudges you. The Holy Spirit is called in Greek the *parakletos*, which may literally be translated "advocate," "teacher," and "comforter."

The Holy Spirit is our closest companion. He is the comforter and guide Jesus promised he would send when he spoke with his disciples in John 14. The Holy Spirit lives in us and reveals God to us. There are times when he will bring to mind particular thoughts, persons, or ideas or even reveal things suddenly to give you understanding. The best friend you ever had probably knew you as well as, or possibly better than, anyone else. A friend that close is a confidant. You are secure with that person and know they have your best in mind.

The Holy Spirit is even closer and more intuitive! Because he was involved in the designing process of your entire being, he knows your wiring and how best to get concepts across to you. Speaking personally, sometimes as I am working or going about my day, I will, seemingly unaccountably, get a picture of someone in my mind, perhaps someone I haven't thought about in a while. I have learned that, when those things happen, the Holy Spirit is getting my attention and most likely wants me to consider what to do with that picture in my mind.

I have learned to ask the Holy Spirit, "Should I pray for this person?" or "Should I text them or call them?' Whatever nudge I get, I follow. The response is almost always positive, and I can be assured that the Spirit of God orchestrated the situation for his purposes. Most often the person will respond that the timing was perfect and express appreciation for the encouragement. Why? Because the Holy Spirit is the one leading, and I am simply noticing what he is doing.

That really is the point here: that we need to notice what the Holy Spirit is doing. Sometimes we have our minds buried in the natural world around us and become lost in our own headspace so that we don't pay attention to the subtle leading of the Spirit. I would invite you to begin to ask the Lord to teach you to hear his voice and respond to his promptings. The Holy Spirit is waiting for us to ask him for those things he desires for us, and for others through us—making it vital that we know his voice and how he leads us.

Erik, a friend I meet with regularly, told me a while back that he never had dreams. Erik had been reading about various characters in the Scriptures who had memorable and highly meaningful dreams, and he was beginning to wonder if that was possible for him. I suggested to him over lunch one day, "Why don't you ask the Holy Spirit to allow you to have dreams from him?" He thought about that for a minute and said, "You know what, I think I'm going to do that. Do you think it will happen?" I replied, "I guess you'll know before long!"

No kidding, within a few weeks when we met for lunch again, he announced, "You'll never believe some of the dreams I've been having!" He went on to explain some of the things he was dreaming about. God was giving him wonderful dreams about himself and the people he loved. He is thrilled to have meaningful dreams from time to time, and this has brought fresh creativity into his life and his faith. What is it that you would like to ask the Spirit to reveal to you? Ask him. Then wait as the Holy Spirit opens your understanding and reveals new thoughts and creative ways to notice his leading.

Learning How the Spirit of God Can Lead Us

I will never forget the way God showed me how to ask him for anything—no matter how incredible the request might seem to me. My family and I were on our way to work at a sports camp in Northern Michigan when our car broke down about ten miles from the camp. Fortunately, we were at a roadside rest area. One of the camp clinicians, Shelby, an Olympic gold medalist who taught at the camp, happened to stop at that rest area. When he saw us broken down, he jumped in to help, and we hauled my disabled car to the camp. Being handy with car engines, he found the problem, a belt that had snapped. We found an auto parts store in a town nearby, where we picked up the parts needed.

Back at the camp he began to try to place the long serpentine belt in place, but he became frustrated and could not understand how it was woven through the engine. He looked at me and said, "Well, God gave the mind to man to invent this car, so let's ask him—let's pray." We stood together with our hands on the car, and he prayed, "Lord, you created the minds of the men who made automobiles. You can give us wisdom about how to put this belt on correctly. Thank you for helping us to do that. Amen."

And just like that, when he opened his eyes after praying, he said, "Hey, I just thought of something. I think we can flip the belt around the other way." He placed it differently around a couple of pulleys, and there it was . . . fitted perfectly for its purpose.

That lesson taught me so much about waiting on the Holy Spirit and asking the Spirit of God key questions. To listen to the Holy Spirit begins by being dedicated to God's Word. I realize that we have covered this earlier, but the subject requires going one step further at this point. If you are studying God's Word, which constitutes his voice to you, you have put yourself in the position to hear him through his Word and to be directed by his Spirit.

One thing I've discovered by reading and studying the Word on a daily basis is that what I read and study becomes a message to me from the Lord, a message that becomes part of what the Lord uses, through me, to convey to other people. When I go into a meeting with someone, I like to have in mind a Scripture or idea from the Bible that I believe will be pertinent to our discussion. Quite often what God puts on my mind for another person comes directly from what I have read and studied earlier that day. So often it's a direct hit that speaks to what that individual is dealing with, going through, or wanting an answer for. This connection continually shows me, and others, that God knows how to give us what we need when we need it.

I'm going to illustrate how the Holy Spirit leads with a bit more of an extreme example.

A few years back during the COVID-19 lockdown, I received a message one Monday morning from a former student: "We are out of food, and my dad doesn't get paid until Friday. Do you have $20 to spare so I can buy some food?" I responded, "Can you meet me at Family Fare (a local grocery store)? We can get you what you need." I did not get a reply. Later that night, around 8:00 p.m., however, I received a message, "Hey man, I'm at Family Fare." While it was interesting that it took quite a while for this response, I immediately responded that I would be there in ten minutes.

The young person I met at the store did not look anything like the young girl I had taught years earlier. There appeared to be a young man standing in front of me with similar facial features as the girl I had known from school. Nevertheless, we grabbed a shopping cart and began to fill it with everything needed for the week ahead. During our shopping trip this former student began to unfold a story of heartbreak, mistakes, and a transition surgery a few years earlier.

After we had driven with the groceries back to the young person's house, we sat in the driveway and wrapped up the conversation with an understanding that I would help again as the need arose. I asked if I could pray. There was a somewhat hesitant yes, so I prayed a prayer of blessing over this family and thanked God for the way he always seems to provide, especially in hard situations. I was asked whether I could be contacted again, and I gave a very positive, "Yes, of course!"

Here is the point of this story.

As I drove away, I asked the Lord what the situation was all about, why a young person who now claimed to be transgender would get ahold of me and how I then should proceed. The thoughts that came to mind, which I absolutely believe were the Holy Spirit's words to me, were simply, "The Word of God." I took that to mean that my foundation for working with this young person must always be from the vantage point of Scripture. This also means that, because Jesus *is* the Word of God, I must always point to him.

Since that initial meeting we have had countless opportunities to meet and to talk, and I have been asked some very pointed questions, to which I have always responded from the Word, with patience, love, and hope. Our relationship has been very positive, and my consistent motivation has been to demonstrate that true identity exists, as declared in Scripture, through the transforming power of Jesus Christ. This has been well received. The journey is not over, and there will be more opportunities to help and walk alongside this young person, with Jesus leading.

The Holy Spirit is showing us that, no matter what the context of a relationship or how messy a topic or endeavor may be, he will always lead us to understanding and truth. The Holy Spirit is limitless, and his intellect and ability will show us in each situation how to proceed.

As we endeavor to listen to the Spirit of God, there is a scriptural precedent I want to offer you that can help tremendously when making decisions. To understand this principle, let's look at Philippians 4:6, 7: "Do not be anxious about anything, but in every situation, by prayer and petition, with thanksgiving, present your requests to God. And the peace of God, which transcends all understanding, will guard your hearts and minds in Christ Jesus."

Okay, so how does this work in making practical, everyday decisions? First, you consider the things you are choosing between. Take one of two possibilities and begin to pray about them, asking the Lord for his direction and will. Then thank the Lord that he hears you and wants to give you direction, knowing that he wants you to know his will. Thanking God takes you out of worry and frustration into the reality that God knows what you need to decide and will lead you. The next verse, Philippians 4:6, tells us to petition, which means to continue to ask. The principle here is that you ask until you have peace, as in verse 7: The peace of God that transcends all understanding. Next, think about the first direction you prayed about and consider whether there is peace there. You may not know immediately, and that is okay.

The second step is to consider another direction you could go and walk through the same process in prayer. At the end of that prayer, again, determine whether you have peace about that direction. This may require a longer wait time than you expect. For example, several years ago I was asked to take the leadership of the wrestling division of a ministry I participated in. Initially, I knew it was a slam dunk. I had a desire to do it, the ability, and a plethora of new ideas.

Yet, after talking with my wife, we agreed I would pray about it. In fact, I had a slight hesitation about moving forward with an immediate yes, a whisker-sized hesitation that caused me to wait and pray. For the first week, I felt nothing but excitement about the opportunity. The next week was much the same, and I thought, "I should just call and accept this position." Somehow, though, I knew I should wait. We really need to pay attention to those red flags or cautions the Holy Spirit uses to get our attention.

During the third week, I had a bit of uneasiness about taking the position. No apparent reasons, just uneasiness. Note: This lack of peace in one direction should signal us that we are receiving an alert from the Lord.

In the fourth week, I heard a very pronounced "Stop!" when it came to accepting the position. Again, I was given no important reasons, just an internal no. At last, at the end of the fourth week, I told my wife I had no peace about accepting the position. I made the call and simply said, "Thank you for the offer, but I cannot accept the position at this time."

Sometimes a lack of peace, or a feeling of unrest, points us to a direction that will lead to peace. Many times, my wife and I have waited to sense peace within ourselves and then relied on the feeling of unrest to help us steer clear of a wrong decision. God used a lack of peace as an indicator of what he was showing us. By the way, you don't perfect this process—you practice it. That's right, practice. God wants us to learn, experientially, to trust his leadership by following the Holy Spirit in prayer. God is a big God with infinite mercy toward us as we come to learn how to follow his lead. He is big enough to take our limited abilities and help us to discern his will!

The Other Mission

"Shadow Mission" is a term coined by John Ortberg in his book *Overcoming Your Shadow Mission*. The gist is that we have each been assigned a mission from God. When we don't recognize that intended mission, we will adopt another, a "shadow mission." Or we may very well know our singular mission but still get caught up in a shadow mission—that self-chosen alternate we adopt that takes us away from our true ministry, our calling. The book is compelling and insightful, especially in that it points out the fact that we all have blind spots in our lives we need to be aware of.

When we set out to make disciples, following the Lord's command from Matthew 28 through the ways in which we are wired and gifted, there will be many opportunities to get off track and even possibly sabotage our own mission. A shadow mission can be a slight miscalculation on our part or something secretive and insidious that is actually motivating us.

The point is that when we begin to serve in our ministry areas it is vital for us to remain accountable to others and let them see into our lives and ministries and help us determine what we should be doing—and not doing. Let me ask you this very important question: Who knows the singular mission you are called to? And is that person (hopefully more than one) helping to keep you focused without distraction on that singular mission?

Stay Singular and Enjoy It!

The ministry I lead is called 99:1 Ministries. My singular mission is to make disciples, and the way I go about doing that is usually one-to-one—me and another person—one at a time. Unless, of course, I'm meeting with a couple in a marriage or pre-marriage relationship. We meet, we talk, and we walk together. Early on the Lord had to slow me down and keep me focused on this singular mission because there are so many other possibilities out there for Christian ministry and service.

When I served in leadership at various churches over the years, I conducted or facilitated Bible studies, youth groups, discipleship groups, men's studies, group mission trips, and group retreats. At the time I enjoyed them and felt that they were making a difference for many who attended those events and groups. However, I now move within and work on the mission I have received—making myself available for one-to-one meetings during the week. This is my calling at this time (along with a bit of writing here and there...).

When I consider what else I could do and begin to think and plan outside my singular mission, my energy and ability get diffused and misused. I have to come back to walking with people individually. My wife is the number one person who keeps me on track with regard to my commitment to the ministry we have received. She knows me and knows what we have agreed to. Whether it's ministry with people or decisions about finances and spending or about where we or I will go, she is the number one person who holds me accountable.

I also have a mentors who know my calling and giftings as close friends. They are able to give me counsel and correction whenever needed. I have several friends who know me and know what I am called to do. I meet with and talk with them regularly. They ask insightful and sometimes very directional, correctional questions. I want, need, and appreciate this help. I look forward to it. If you ever feel as if you want to go it alone, "doing your thing" without answering to others, immediately tell someone. This urge is from the enemy, who wants to get you alone and into a shadow mission.

What is your singular mission? Can you explain it in a sentence or two, or do you need to take some time to write down and define the mission God has given you in order to make disciples? I want to encourage you to take time right now to express in written form the mission God has called you to. Make it clear and plain. Pray as you go, asking the Spirit of God to show you clearly what he has come alongside to help you with. Then decide who you need explain your calling to. Be open to their questions; they may help you refine your thinking and firm up the details of your calling.

One of the most convicting questions I was ever asked about my mission as a teacher was posed by my son Zach. One day Zach came home from high school and, in a very disturbed tone, asked me, "Dad, aren't teachers supposed to do more than just teach their subject? Shouldn't they all care about the students in their classrooms?" I responded, "Yes, I believe teachers are supposed to be concerned for all of their students, and, speaking personally, I try to keep that as my first priority, although I want to teach the content well also."

Zach responded, "Yeah I get that, but how can a teacher stand in front of a class, look around their classroom, notice that a student is depressed and checked out, and do or say nothing about it?" My next response was, "I think every teacher must care enough about their students to step in when they notice that something doesn't seem right, but I'm also speaking as someone who wants to represent the Lord Jesus Christ in a classroom."

Zach then asked, "How many of my teachers do you think are Christians?" "Well, Zach," I replied, "that's impossible to know, although I'm sure many of them would consider themselves to be Christians." In a very frustrated voice my son stated, "Well, some don't seem like it because I had a girl sitting next to me in class with her head down. She was obviously very distraught and depressed, and the teacher went through the whole class period and said nothing to her." Zach has an immense sense of justice and compassion when it comes to people. It wasn't long before he befriended this young lady, brought the girl to our house. and did everything in his power to make a difference in her life.

My son Zach's deep concern and pointed questions had me evaluating the reality of my singular mission. I had to reflect whether I was really on point with the mission of showing Jesus Christ to my students or in any way sidetracked by the shadow missions I could pursue—perhaps approval, professionalism, perfectionism, or a host of other possibilities? Zach's frustration and sense of justice caused me to reaffirm the reason I was in the classroom and make a concerted effort to show the love and grace of Jesus Christ to my students.

Shadow missions. The context might be a classroom, office, courtroom, or restaurant or in a marriage or as a parent. Shadow missions keep us from seeing what God sees and responding as God responds, wanting us to follow suit. We must stay open and accountable to others and to God so we can keep the number one mission number one.

Chapter 16

Interruptions and Noticing

Teaching Disciples of the Lord Jesus to Notice Possibilities

You no doubt have seen this word in a couple of forms throughout this book: "Notice." I emphasize this term because it denotes the way in which we should pay attention to the ways the Lord is working around us. When we are busy with our day, our plans, or our work life, taking notice can at times be an interruption that awakens us to an awareness of God's work.

It seems obvious that Jesus's disciples were put off by interruptions. After all, they were walking with the Messiah! Certainly, he should not be disturbed or interrupted, right? At least that is the way they often perceived things. For example, blind Bartimaeus (Mark 10:46-52) cried out as Jesus and his disciples walked by. The disciples tried to shut this guy up, but Jesus stopped them and had them call Bartimaeus over.

The same is true for the woman who had been suffering from a 12-year hemorrhage (Mark 5:25–32). Jesus was en route to heal Jairus's daughter when he noticed that someone had touched him. With another life and death situation in front of him, he took the time for this woman. Many more scenarios show Jesus's pattern of stopping when interrupted and noticing what his Father was doing around him. In fact, it would appear that interruptions were what prompted Jesus to notice that his Father had work for him to do.

In Ephesians 5:15 the apostle Paul writes, "See then that ye walk *circumspectly*, not as fools, but as wise, redeeming the time" (emphasis added). The word *circumspect* comes from two roots—*circum*, meaning circle, and *specere*, which means to look. The idea is to look around yourself cautiously, prudently, or vigilantly. Notice the environment and activity around you. Let me share an example.

On a recent Saturday morning, my wife and I were heading a couple of hours away to her dad's house, where she was bringing food, as she does every couple of weeks. Just before we left, Anne mentioned that she needed hamburger buns to take with her, so I offered, "I'll grab those from the store and be right back."

I jumped into the car and headed to the store a mile away. My plan was just to run in and run out. I hustled quickly through the store, grabbed the hamburger buns my wife had asked me to get, and noticed a sale on packs of bottled water. I knew we needed some, so I picked one up and, feeling its heft, decided not to go through the express checkout. Instead, I went to one of the conveyors with a cashier.

As I set down the water bottles and fumbled around for my credit card, I was interrupted by the cooing of an infant—a cute baby probably nine months old or so in a baby seat in the cart in front of me. His babbling and bright blue eyes jolted me from my hamburger bun mission, and I looked up. His young mother, I noticed, was handing the cashier a paper receipt from bottle returns. I looked at the items she was buying: baby formula and baby diapers.

It took only seconds to surmise that this young mother was using returned soda cans to pay for the formula and diapers she needed. She obviously was having some trouble affording her baby's needs. I understood that the Lord was perhaps wanting me to act on his behalf, so I looked up at the young lady and said, "I don't mean to intrude, but may I pay for your groceries?"

Immediately she looked shocked and blurted, "No . . . why would you do that?" The cashier chimed in, saying, "Yes, honey, you should save this receipt for some other time you need something." I was glad to have the support. I said again, "Really, it's no trouble. I'd like to do that for you." As she nodded her "okay," I handed my credit card to the cashier as the girl stared at me.

When I turned to face her direction, she stated, "This morning I asked God if he was real and wondered if I should even believe in him anymore." She spoke with a question in her voice. With all the compassion I could muster, I replied, "God sees you, and he knows you and your baby son. He is for you, and I hope you now understand that he is answering your question."

I asked her baby's name, and hers as well. I was charmed by the smile on this little fellow's face. Then suddenly she stepped closer and quietly shared, "The reason I have him is that I was raped." She wanted to explain a bit more as the cashier and I both listened. She stared at me as though she was realizing that God was at work and that she could trust. I asked, "How old are you?"

"I am in high school," she replied.

I was quiet for a moment as the last statement sank in. I then asked, "Could I pray for you and your son?" She gave a very willing nod. I leaned forward, and the cashier joined us as well as we bowed our heads. I asked God to let this young mother know that she is always seen by him and dearly loved, to lead her to always know that he is available and has her best in mind, that her little boy is a blessing, and that he would have a destiny purposed by God, not by circumstances. As we finished praying, the cashier stepped around the counter and gave her a hug. The young customer went on her way with a smile and a sense of assurance.

When I returned home, I walked into my living room feeling overwhelmed by what had occurred. I wept at the weight of the event that had just taken place and thanked God for interrupting my morning mission to hastily purchase hamburger buns. God tends to remind me fairly often that he has a big mission that supersedes my little missions in life.

What if I hadn't noticed this young lady in front of me in that line? What if I had been so distracted by my "mission" of securing hamburger buns and water that I had missed that moment of need and desperation for this young lady and her son? I need to notice. We need to notice. God is at work. He never stops. We are his hands and feet . . . and his pocketbook at times as well. We are the mechanics, builders, surgeons, techies, cashiers, Uber drivers, and everything else our Father in heaven needs for us to be.

Let the rivers flow . . .

Interruptions. Most people I know hate interruptions. If you are a person who likes to get after tasks and accomplish things efficiently, then interruptions can get you sidelined. But God relishes interruptions, and he loves to interrupt us!

One of the ways Jesus responded to interruptions was with compassion, a God-directed response to something happening around us that needs our attention. Noticing what is happening and studying our environment, "being in the moment," can allow compassion to arise so that we will respond properly to what God is showing us to do.

Check out the following scene and take note of how Jesus responded with compassion. In Matthew 14:12 Jesus was told that his cousin and partner in ministry, John the Baptizer, had been beheaded by King Herod. Jesus's response was to tell his disciples that they needed to get away for a time of rest. They had been meeting the needs of thousands and had to have been weary.

Jesus, fully God and fully human, must have been heartbroken beyond words. But his response was to get into a boat with his beleaguered disciples to sail to the other side of the lake, . . . only to find that the people they had ministered to, in the thousands, had followed them. Matthew records, "When Jesus landed and saw a large crowd, he had compassion on them and healed their sick" (Matthew 14:14).

If we will take the time to notice our surroundings and what is taking place around us, we will in the pattern of our Savior be moved to compassion at the right times and witness God changing lives.

Chapter 17

Discipleship in Your Family

Possibly the hardest place to be a disciple and to disciple others is in our immediate families. They know us best and see the "real" us, all the time. As we grow and change as disciples of the Lord Jesus, sometimes the changes aren't apparent; in fact, sometimes we are regarded according to our past tendencies. Discipleship has to do with how you lead yourself while you exercise leadership in your family and how you follow Jesus Christ.

When I was a fresh follower of Christ, just one week into my relationship with Jesus, I wrote a letter to my family explaining my newfound relationship with Jesus Christ. While my family had attended church, we had never been centered on Jesus Christ, and I wanted us as a family to go all in. I pleaded with my family to turn to Jesus Christ, the only way of salvation, and shared the details of my experience in learning of God's love through the death and resurrection of his beloved Son on our behalf. I pleaded with them to turn to Jesus because I wanted to see them all in heaven one day.

When I sent that impassioned letter at the beginning of my journey with Christ, I didn't realize that I would be setting up what it looked like to follow him as a disciple, and I certainly didn't recognize that I was laying down for my family an example of what a disciple acted like. Yet that was the reality. In practicing discipleship—and that is truly what we do—we are embarking on a path that will be long and arduous, with many ups and downs. The ups are incredible highs, while the downs can be very discouraging. In family, that's the way it works! I look back now and see that I exhibited a very imperfect witness. I was bold and judgmental. Yet God, working through his Spirit, was in the process of changing me—and worked in my family-in spite of me.

Many of you are trying to live as a disciple within your family. I want to encourage you to continue on, pressing in to all that Jesus has called you to participate in, knowing that your imperfections do not undermine the work of God. There are no perfect witnesses, but only broken people experiencing the healing and restoration God provides.

Whether you are the disciple in your family or are leading a family and training your children, there are some nuggets of truth and experiential advice I can offer that may prove helpful.

1. Your life example is a greater witness than your words.
2. Your words do count.
3. Walk with humility.
4. Pursue Christ above all else.
5. Remain teachable.
6. Live selflessly.

Your Life Example Has Greater Impact than Your Words

In education we have a phrase that most teachers know well. Maybe you've heard it: "They don't care how much you know until they know how much you care." This is never truer than in your family context. Being a witness and disciple in a family is hard, because home is the place where we desire to rest, and we may end up trying to relax at the times we need to be most aware and alert.

Remember our conversation about interruptions? My experience is that the interruptions happen most often in our family settings. Wow, does this expose our selfishness! My wife, Anne, has grown in selflessness faster than I have over time and has been a continual model for me to watch and emulate as she serves Christ with self-sacrifice. One of the most challenging statements I once heard from a friend, as he was referring to his wife, was, "My goal each day is to serve my wife more than she serves me." I don't believe we should keep score in our marriages, but the overall challenge is to lead by the idea of outdoing our spouse in service—going further.

How to live your witness.

Some years ago, I was reading in John 13 about Jesus washing his disciples' feet. The passage reads, "When he had finished washing their feet, he [Jesus] put on his clothes and returned to his place. 'Do you understand what I have done for you?' he asked them. 'You call me "Teacher" and "Lord," and rightly so, for that is what I am. Now that I, your Lord and teacher, have washed your feet, you also should wash one another's feet. I have set you an example that you should do as I have done for you. Very truly I tell you, no servant is greater than his master, nor is a messenger greater than the one who sent him. Now that you know these things, you'll be blessed if you do them'" (John 13:12–17).

I asked the Lord to show me how to apply this teaching to my life, and the question that came to mind was, "What does washing feet look like in my family?" What I thought about was this: washing feet took Jesus to a place of lowliest service, even though he was the highest leader. What things could or should I do that, typically, I don't have to do? In other words, for me as a husband and father, are there are certain things I have learned that I don't have to do because of the division of labor in our home, as my wife and I have determined together the regular tasks we will each take on? I immediately thought of laundry, cleaning bathrooms, and especially taking care of miscellaneous tasks quickly when I see a need.

We all want rest and relaxation, but when we rest at the cost of our selfless serving, our desire to "chill" may in fact be too high of a priority. I have found that there were things I really didn't want to do but that I needed to have a better attitude about. I needed to live an example of the selfless Jesus. This was a turning point for me in that the idea of "washing feet" became a mirror for me—and I didn't like the reflection I saw. I knew I could do a much better job of being selfless and humble, volunteering to take on many tasks that would be a blessing to my wife and family. Maybe you should make a similar assessment for yourself; Are there things you could do to make your home more of a haven of rest for others?

Another example of how *our life speaks louder than our words*: for many years when my kids were young my wife and I had devotions with each of them. These sessions were valuable in myriad ways. They learned about Bible history and the story of Jesus—in our case right along with us. Questions were asked, we were able to engage in in-depth dialogues at various points, and I believe we enjoyed the process overall. I look back and I am glad we took the time to be involved in a devotional experience with our kids. While at different points the experience was hit-or-miss, I remember very special moments along the way.

Now that my kids are adults, I realize that the most important "devotional" they need is to observe my wife and me: devoted to the Lord every day over these years, as well as to each other and to each of them and their families. Devotion is seen by the examples set . . . or not set. When the Lord determines that our time on earth has been completed, the memories my kids will have of Anne and me remaining faithful to the Lord, faithful to each other, and faithful to them is the impression that will last. Our lives truly do matter more than our words.

Parenting and walking in discipleship with your family is an organic experience of trial and error (or *trial and terror*, as I sometimes refer to it). Finding the rhythm for your family and acknowledging how you and your wife are uniquely wired are vital moving forward as you endeavor to lead with devotional experiences.

There are many great models for us to follow as foundational disciplines, but the key is not to fall into a religious routine but to watch closely over our own walk and be on the alert for key moments to impart truth.

I have relied on Deuteronomy 6:6, 7 on many occasions as a way to understand how to teach our children: "These commandments that I give you today are to be on your hearts. Impress them on your children. Talk about them when you sit at home and when you walk along the road, when you lie down and when you get up." The relational offering of the words and ways of God is gentle and persuasive when shared in this context. Consider the following with me:

- **When you sit at home.** There are many opportunities to interject biblical thinking as we are at home with our families. Many times, these take place especially in the interruptions and conflicts that occur which allow us to teach the way that the Lord would have us act and respond in any and every situation. As children are growing it can be exhausting to continue the pace of teaching and instruction. It helps to know that our primary responsibility is to raise our children with the understanding of the ways the Lord has designed us and how he desires us to learn. God is very patient with us and understands the process well; after all, he has been teaching and instructing us with love and patience as we have been growing in his grace and truth!
- **When you walk by the road.** This setting speaks of a father or mother on a patient journey with a son or daughter, walking together with them in relationship and discussing the aspects and character of God as they amble along. Maybe it's about noticing something in creation—the foliage, the wildlife, the sky. Maybe it's a setting in the city with the lights, the noises, and the smells all eliciting curious questions about life, people, and God's will. Hard questions are sometimes brought up as you walk or drive together
- **When you lie down.** Isn't it incredible that, when you are putting your kids to bed, exhausted from the day's activities, the questions so often

seem to tumble out? Embrace this challenge even if you feel yourself wanting only to endure it—sink into the moments. One day you will look back at those moments spent kneeling next to your son or daughter's bed—or lying alongside them, giving yourself to the setting, to the questions, and to the process Deuteronomy 6 has offered—spending precious time setting a concrete foundation of understanding about the Lord.

Ever read Proverbs 22:6—"Train up a child in the way he should go, and even when he is old, he will not depart from it"? This is a remarkable promise that helps us see that the training we embark on with our family holds tremendous promise and rewards. However, for many the fruit will not be readily seen. We need to consider that the Word of God, along with glimpses of his character, woven throughout our lives is indelibly imprinted but has its own timetable for growth.

Some of you reading this will have, or will have had, heartaches with regard to your children, their direction, and their decisions. We play the long game. I am always encouraged by this truth from James, the apostle and half brother of Jesus: "Be patient then, brothers and sisters, until the Lord's coming. See how the farmer waits for the land to yield its valuable crop, patiently waiting for the autumn and spring rains. You too, be patient and stand firm, because the Lord's coming is near."

Okay, how does this apply to your kids? First, the autumn rains saturate the fields, soaking them with the water that will begin the next season's growth. As a parent you have watered. You know you have set a foundation of the Word of God in the soil of your kids' lives. That is vitally important, and you can trust that whatever you have shared and prayed about with them over the years constitutes water that has already saturated their being.

The seed has been sown, and the autumn rains have done their part. Then come the spring rains, without which there will be no germination. Please consider carefully whether the spring rains might have yet to come, recalling that, while you are praying and at times questioning God and what he is doing as the master gardener, he is waiting for the perfect time to send those spring rains into the lives of your children. If the rains come too early, the ground can be overly saturated. If they come too late, on the other hand, the crop will fail. God is impeccable in his timing. Trust these words of Scripture: "See how the farmer waits for the land to yield its valuable crop, patiently waiting for the autumn and spring rains."

- *When you get up.* "Because of the Lord's great love we are not consumed, for his compassions never fail. They are new every morning. Great is your faithfulness" (Lamentations 3:22, 23). These verses are a staple in our home and in my mind. Whenever the days are long and hard and we are disappointed, we can rely on the refreshing water of this truth: the Lord's mercies are new every morning. What hope! What encouragement! God knows the possibilities of your next morning. There will be new adventures. He is limitless in what he can offer in any fresh new day.

In full disclosure, I look back and see that at many times during my child-raising years, I did not have the view that God had anything new on the way. I had work to do, and sometimes it was hard raising my kids. I know this sounds negative, but that is truly where my mind went on many occasions. Some days were so filled with work and drudgery that I failed to see, or foresee, the many mercies accompanying each new each morning.

Without recognizing it, I chose to focus on the things that were hard instead of looking at even these circumstances as blessings and opportunities. I know that my kids could have been more blessed if I had held up the principles of Lamentations 3:22, 23 as the way to approach each new day. I have learned a lot over the years, and one of the most valuable truths in life is to greet each person, each family member, each new day, with a smile and expectation of good! Please accept my invitation, based on years of experience, to see the world, your life, and your kids in terms of hope and possibility. This approach is unmatched in starting the day with your children. Indeed, they will "arise and call [you] blessed!" (Proverbs 31:28).

Having established this reality—that our lives speak more loudly than our words—let me emphasize that there are many outstanding devotionals to use with your kids. Sharing this excellent material as the basis for your devotional time with them works best when you blend in your own actions and words, because *your words do count.*

Yet nothing compares to reading directly from the Word of God, with you as the commentator. Bible character studies can be an incredible source of insight, inspiration, and growth. Many Bible characters demonstrated remarkable ups and downs, strengths, callings, and weaknesses, just as we do. People like Abraham, Sarah, Isaac, Rachel, Moses, Rahab, Samson,

David, Bathsheba, Mary Magdalene, Paul, Peter, and others offer dynamics we can relate to and learn from.

One of the devotionals my wife and I relied on, and that is still available, is titled *Keys for Kids*. The stories and scriptural lessons in this series are combined with great questions that spur thinking, promoting a biblical response to a variety of issues and events. We would usually read a devotion after dinner or before bed. Our kids enjoyed the stories, but even more so the provocative questions they would think about and try to answer. It was challenging and fun at the same time.

That is the ideal to shoot for: make the devotionals fun and thought-provoking. As you read any devotional, the more you attach your own life to it the more you create connections with the stories, and the more real the material becomes for you and your children.

One of the incentives we gave our kids was to memorize Bible verses. Once a verse had been memorized, we would provide a reward of some kind, such as a place to go together as a family to have some fun. When our kids hit the youth group level, it was great for us as parents to be involved at times, either with a fundraiser or in setting up for events. Being there and being involved as other important role models helped our kids in discipleship and has provided a lot of great memories.

Of the myriad devotional activities you can choose to do, there are a couple of unique suggestions that may offer variety. One such pattern is to read each day a proverb corresponding with the particular day of the week, along with a psalm and a chapter from one of the Gospels, Matthew, Mark, Luke, or John. Another idea is to march straight through the New Testament one book at a time. This offers a look at the authors, their purpose for writing, and the truths that can be gleaned as you read their writings with your kids.

Reading books together (timeless suggestions include C. S. Lewis's Chronicles of Narnia series, *The Hiding Place* by Cory Ten Boom, *Pilgrim's Progress for Teens*, and *Kisses from Katie* (a young woman's mission with orphans) can offer unforgettable memories, open up what others have done in following Christ, and offer a view of how a believer can respond in hardships and trials, as well as how to witness and go deeper in following the Lord.

Your kids' teen years can be a time of testing and trials. Please allow me in this context to humbly offer this advice: be an encourager of their identity, of who they are becoming, more than taking on the role or policing their behavior. Your having clear rules and standards is important for setting up teens for responsibility and authority, but when your rules and authority are enforced as of greater importance than the revelation of God's love and mercy and his high valuation for each individual—when the biggest sign in your house has to do with rules rather than character—you set your kids up for failure. Let me explain further.

In Romans 3 Paul taught that the law was given for a period of time until grace was ready to be revealed. Once grace had been revealed, we became children of grace, of freedom—not children of the law. Was the law good? Yes—because it showed us that we couldn't measure up and needed God's love and grace to save us.

Similarly, your kids will never be able to fully keep the rules of your home. Oh, it may look as though they are compliant, but obedience to a law is a behavior that does not necessarily flow from the heart. Such obedience may last for a while, but only a few can maintain the standards long term. What do you call someone who can keep the law, and this includes the rules in your home? A legalist. A law-keeper.

That doesn't necessarily exemplify love, although if you yourself happen to be a legalist, performing every day to keep your set of rules and legal principles, obedience may appear synonymous with love. But true, abiding love comes only through grace. When you can have joy even in the midst of a messy room, with laundry undone and jobs that have been missed—you are walking in grace, and it will permeate your home. In contrast, when you are upset by all that has been missed, when your pleadings and punishments yield no true change, you do well to rethink your mindset and the priorities of your home. "Better to live on a corner of a roof than share a house with a quarrelsome wife [or dad or mom]" (Proverbs 21:9).

Check out these Proverbs to shed light on the climate of your mind and your home:

"The wise in heart are called discerning, and gracious words promote instruction." (Proverbs 16:21)

"Gracious words are a honeycomb, sweet to the soul and healing to the bones." (Proverbs 16:24)
"Better a patient person than a warrior, one with self-control than one who takes a city [or heavily controls their home]. (Proverbs 16:32)

"Whoever would foster love covers over an offense, but whoever repeats the matter separates close friends." (Proverbs 17:9)

"The tongue has the power of life and death, and those who love it will eat its fruit." (Proverbs 18:21)

The words of others count, too.

One of the important aspects in the discipleship of your kids is providing important role models that assist in their growth. For kids to have other trusted adults in their lives is vital. There will be times when our kids need to talk with and confide in someone else. What potential disciple-makers could that be in your sphere of influence? Anne and I have had several. We are blessed to have two brothers-in-law who have been outstanding examples and confidantes to our four sons. Their names are Mike and Dave. They have been involved in every level of my boys' growth into men.

My daughter, Lauren, has her aunts Patty and Sharon as mentors, and for all of my kids, there are others from their youth group years who have made a big impact—Jason, Mandy, and Roger. If you are not sure who is like minded with you and potentially a mentor for your kids, pray for such people to emerge. As the Lord said to Elijah when he thought he was alone in his quest for God, "I reserve seven thousand in Israel—all whose knees have not bowed to Baal" (1 Kings 19:18).

Discipleship Examples of Serving

One of the greatest things you can do with your children lies in the action of serving. Taking your children with you as you go to someone's house to do work—housework, cleaning, fixing something, etc., allows them to see Jesus in action. We are, after all, his hands and feet on this earth. Giving your time periodically and explaining why you are serving others is a key that unlocks the heart. When our kids see the effects of blessing someone, they begin to form a worldview of service and helping others. In Christianity, this is a foundational piece. Making meals for people, visiting those who are down and hurting, and many other examples: these are valuable experiences that allow you to have conversations about why you love and serve people.

One of the people in my life who embodies this Christlike heart for serving is my sister Pam. She tirelessly serves people with meals and visits, counseling and playing music for them with her husband, Robin. Honestly, Pam is the primary person in my life who challenges me to serve from the heart because she is passionate about it and quicker in response than any EMT team available. The kicker—she *never* complains. Wow. Pam is the image of someone washing others' feet. I praise God for her example and the teamwork she and her husband provide where they live. Our kids have seen this for years and witnessed many blessings from their hands. I hope you have a Pam and a Robin in your life as examples. Actually, I hope you become that person in your sphere of influence!

Another way for your kids to see your faith in action is to host people in your home. Your children will see first-hand the blessing of giving your time and space for those who have needs or at least want to spend some time with your family, for fellowship and to learn and grow together. Serving together in your church is yet another outstanding way to walk with your kids in discipleship.

Have you lost touch with one of your kids—perhaps as a teen or an adult? Are you distanced or estranged? Pray. Pray for insight from the Lord as to how to insert yourself back into some form of communication. If there is a closed door, pray that it opens. Pray for other people to enter the life of the one who seems lost or alienated. God sees that one and knows how to bring them to a place of needing him and to usher in those key individuals who can be guides along the way. In Luke 18 Jesus tells of the widow who persists and prevails because she will not stop her annoying plea before a judge. Jesus commended her and called this faith. You may be weary—but don't stop! Continue on, and also find others to agree with you in prayer.

Your Words Do Count

Your conversations about God and the way you represent him by your speech make a lasting impression. Whether you are the disciple or the disciple-maker in your home, your conversation matters! Jesus stated that "the mouth speaks what the heart is full of" (Luke 6:45). What is your point of view—predominately positive or mostly negative? Do you speak with encouragement or criticism? Do your kids hear blessings for your spouse, or put-downs? Their tender hearts form around words and language.

This Scripture should always guide and correct us: "Do not let any unwholesome talk come out of your mouths, but only what is helpful for building others up according to their needs, that it may benefit those who listen" (Ephesians 4:29). Here is another like it: "Do everything without grumbling or arguing" (Philippians 2:14). Words create atmosphere and climate. Words produce life or death. Words validate or demean. Words are what we hear in our ears, our mind, our heart, and our spirit. Words form us.

If the Word of God is living and active, ours should be as well. This includes names we have for our family members, especially our kids. Names should never have a negative connotation attached or implied. Names should build up, not tear down. They give us image and identity. That is why Jesus called Simon "Peter," meaning "little stone." A piece of the rock! That is also why God changed Jacob's name from "deceiver" to "Israel": one who wrestles with God and overcomes.

How can a name make a difference?

When I was a young college athlete, I specifically remember walking down the hallway of the college fieldhouse on my way to wrestling practice and meeting the football coach coming from his office. He called me "Wildman" every time he saw me. Was I a wild man? I was a young college athlete, but whenever he called me Wildman I went into the practice room feeling more like a true athlete than like an untried college kid. I would go out of my way to walk by his office on many occasions just to hear him call me that nickname. That's a great name for a college athlete. Wildman. I loved it, and he inspired me.

Do you really understand what a name can mean? A name is our identity! My name, Jeffrey, means "gracious gift of peace." That makes me understand part of my identity from God—to bring peace and purpose into the lives of others. My wife's name, Anne, means "favor" and "grace." She certainly shows these qualities and offers them without limit to others. We gave our kids special names that likewise confer value and identity.

Jordan means "descending river," bringing life and vitality everywhere and to everyone. He refreshes and nourishes. Caleb means "faithful" and "wholehearted," traits in a warrior. He protects and rescues. Zachary means "The Lord has remembered." God has remembered to love and honor him and to show others that he sees and hears them also. Alex means "leader/defender of men." Again, like a warrior. Protecting, delivering to safety, and leading wisely. Lauren means "wisdom" and "honored." She is indeed honored for the wisdom she offers freely to others.

What does your name mean?

Might I suggest that you look up the meanings of the names you use? Find a positive description and begin to treat people—especially your family—according to the blessings and benefits symbolized by their names. Speak life over them and into them. Speak life also over yourself, my friend. God loves you dearly and wants you to know that he sees you as his precious son or daughter.

Also, when someone—especially in your family—messes up, call them back to their God-given purpose by using the name that means the most. Speak words and a name that is life-giving and purposeful to that one who is lost, down, discouraged, or even willfully sinning. Call them back to God's name for them. Lead them to it by speaking life.

Walk with Humility

For those who live at home as a disciple

Following Jesus as a disciple establishes that which a family will take on in later years as foundational. Standing on the Word of God as ultimate truth, praying, witnessing, worshiping, and being part of the body of Christ—all of these stances and actions are important for families to see and take part in along the way, as each one "tests the waters." Family members will, of course, also see our weaknesses, inconsistencies, and faults, but God is the One who changes us day by day and along the way fulfills his promise, "[Be] confident of this, that he who began a good work in you will carry it on to completion until the day of Christ Jesus" (Philippians 1:6).

Obedience from the heart

One of greatest testimonies we can offer our families is our obedience to the Lord that translates to the way we live with humility, honesty, and integrity. Whenever we can speak with humble honesty, when we have a ready "Yes" when asked to help with things needing to be done, that type of heartfelt obedience changes someone else's perspective. Joseph was a great example of this type of heartfelt obedience. Even though he was sold into slavery, lied about, imprisoned, and abandoned, in every place he found himself he obeyed authority, obeyed God, and ultimately was blessed. Although you may have to endure hardship for a time, maintain your obedience as from the heart, blessing people out of a heart for God. He will lead you, and you will one day see the fruit of your obedience!

Pursue Christ above All Else

In your family and elsewhere, the precedent you set by making your time with the Lord a first priority will be an incredible testimony to others around you. My roommate Dorr began this example for me when I was learning about Jesus. Dorr got up at the break of day, read his Bible, and went through a prayer folder. Looking back, I saw his character becoming solid and consistent through these disciplines. When I became a new believer, this also became my first priority because the model had been clear—this is what a disciple does. It sets up the foundation.

When my best friend Jeff learned about my new relationship with Jesus, he met with me frequently and added to the example Dorr had established. Jeff taught me how to study the Bible by understanding context. He taught me how to read for meaning and to let the Scriptures do the teaching through the Holy Spirit's leadership. He taught me how to use a commentary and what cross-referencing was about: comparing Scriptures.

Jeff taught me how to memorize the Word of God, and he taught me to pray. We prayed together, and I learned how to seek God in prayer. Jeff didn't pray soft prayers—he was passionate and prayed from the Word of God. His example was powerful! I learned to pray in my home and over my home and for family members—to do so every day and to prevail in prayer, to continue on in the practice, not letting up. These brothers set an example of making Christ first priority, and it greatly influenced my life and shaped it in many important ways.

In your home, you may be on your own as a witness or in family leadership. Either way, making Christ a first priority is individual because Jesus wants to move not only *in* you but also *through* you. Saturate yourself in the things of Christ. Learn to worship. Sing. You may not have a great voice, but you can at least make a joyful noise! By the way, praise breaks strongholds—in you and in others. When there is music and song there is life and vitality. Just a note—don't be an annoyance. If your singing hinders another's peace and quiet—make a joyful noise "to yourself." Put on your headphones or earbuds!

Remain Teachable

For me as a coach, one of the aspects of working with people I have been intrigued by is how coachable or teachable they often are. Being teachable is a trait that reveals a person's heart and desire to grow. Someone who is teachable is a joy to work with. On the other hand, someone who is a know-it-all or defensive is hard to work with, and it can be really tough to gear up mentally to help such a person. They short-circuit their opportunities to grow because of an aversion to hearing from someone else.

By the way, being teachable can be learned. Being open to advice and instruction is a skill, even while it is also an attitude and a character trait. When you begin to see others as participating in your growth and development, knowing that God is using someone for your benefit and the benefit of other people through you, the big picture opens up, and you see the blessing of the teaching and training that people provide.

This is especially true in discipleship. If I am being honest, 95 percent of the people I walk with in discipleship are a joy. They want to be on a discipleship journey because they value the relationship, the camaraderie, and the constructive advice and see them as necessary for their growth.

However, there are those individuals who, whenever we talk, are adversarial. They are negative or critical, make excuses, and quite often do not take ownership of their mistakes or attitudes and frequently blame others. That's a lot of negative stuff for us to wade through. Yet God wades through my "stuff" as well and waits for me on many occasions to have an open and teachable heart. I can be an unteachable student at times, and awareness of this helps me to be patient and understanding of others. I get it . . . usually!

Live Selflessly

I saved this for last because it embodies all the first five points I've written about. To live selflessly means to submit to God your life, your wants, and the things you think you need for your comfort. David wrote in Psalm 23:1, "The LORD is my shepherd, I lack nothing." When I apply that to myself—and I would encourage you to consider yourself in this, too, there is truly nothing I need. God has taken care of it all.

We cannot fix or change many of the circumstances in our lives. But we can be content. We have food and shelter, transportation when we need it, and work to do. And the list goes on . . . You and I really don't need anything. Oh, we think we do, and we usually work quite hard to make our lives more comfortable, but there is nothing we really need. We are in God's hands.

If the life within us were suddenly taken away, where would we be? If you are a follower of Jesus Christ, you would be in the presence of God. Eternity in his presence would begin where he dwells. Know that he is faithful, fully capable of caring for our families and friends without our help. He has done that for billions of people for all of history, and he is committed to continuing his caring and nurturing forever.

Our wants and desires keep our eyes fixed on ourselves and not on those around us. Living selflessly means giving up some of our rights and looking to the benefit of others. The presence of the Spirit of God moves wonderfully where selfless living takes place, but he is quenched and the fire is put out when our gaze is turned inward.

Consider what Paul wrote to the Philippian Christians: "Do nothing out of selfish ambition or vain conceit. Rather, in humility value others above yourselves, not looking to your own interests but each of you to the interests of others" (Philippians 2:3, 4). This makes the point pretty clearly: drop your personal agenda and look at what someone else needs.

Conviction and Convincing

When we live with the focus of being God's hands and feet for others, when we respond to the needs of others and listen well, especially when we could do something else—in other words, when we go the extra mile, show up to help, or enable someone to get work and life done because we are involved—Jesus is the One who shows up, and his presence is noticed because we live like him. Conviction takes place. We and those we serve are convicted by the Spirit of God that we are sharing his love. That kind of conviction lets love become tangible. It is convincing as well. We and others walk away convinced of God being real and good.

How powerful is the church—the body of the Lord Jesus Christ—when we live to love and serve others. One of the greatest testimonies of the church of Jesus Christ being valuable is the way followers of Christ have offered simple acts of mercy and grace that have blessed people all over the world and changed lives. The feeding programs, the organizations that mobilize for disaster relief, those that work to mitigate human trafficking and the atrocities of the sex-slave industry, people who take time to walk through hospitals visiting and praying for the sick—all bring the light and love of Jesus Christ into dark places. Locally, youth groups that mobilize to gather clothes and shoes for those in poverty, spend time in mentorship of younger kids, or find ways to bless families by doing work that needs to be done, all show that the love of Jesus is real and tangible.

My daughter, Lauren, is an example of someone who lives selflessly and finds ways to show the love of Jesus. As a teenager she worked at a senior memory care center, taking care of the needs of individuals who were nearing the end of life. Many had no one else to visit them. One Christmas Lauren came home and said, "I did it—I made it to all of the patients' rooms with cards!"

I remarked, "That's incredible—how did you do that in an evening while you were working?" Lauren replied that she had stayed after work until she had seen them all—all thirty-seven of them. When I asked her how she had found the time to write out all thirty-seven cards, let alone the funds to purchase them, her reply was, "Oh, I didn't buy them—I made them." Tears welled up in my eyes as I saw Jesus poured out through my daughter, preparing, creating, and writing thirty-seven cards and then walking into each room individually to read the cards to her patients and wish them a Merry Christmas before she left work.

I am humbled and challenged. Lauren certainly watched her mom over the years running to the care of friends, family, and anybody else with any kind of need. There have been more meals made and delivered than I could ever count. There have been more coffees and counsel than I could ever count. But one thing I can count (on) is the way my wife, Anne, looks like Jesus and is my icon of service for the Lord.

Discipleship is selfless service for others. I realize that it takes our time, talent, and treasure, but what do we have those things for, anyway? Jesus shows up through our selfless living.

I had a young person say to me one day, reflecting on the family dysfunction she saw around her, that she was "done" with being involved in their "messes." I reflected on that for a moment and then asked if I could offer a thought. She welcomed anything that would help her figure out her place in God's will, so she was listening.

"I would like you to consider for a moment," I began, "how Jesus, the Lord of heaven, was worshiped and praised in heaven before he came to this earth. He was in glory beyond our imagining. He enjoyed the love and presence of Father God, the fellowship of the Holy Spirit, and perfection everywhere—because he is perfect and his kingdom is perfect.

"Consider Jesus leaving that perfection, the beauty, the honor and the glory to come to this earth and live among us in all of our messes. And he rescued us while we were in our mess. He was mocked, beaten, abused, torn, pierced, and put to death . . . to all of which he submitted willingly to rescue us from the mess of sin. He took our mess upon himself to die with it. We know he rose in new victory over death and hell, so he has power to help us with any mess we're in. Perhaps God is calling you to what is messy—because he is able to sort it out when it appears too much for us. If God is not afraid of a mess, then we shouldn't be, either."

She got it. We need to get it. Discipleship, serving, helping—it's messy business.

One of the examples that helped me understand what serving looks like when the situation is messy came from reading about many Christian martyrs—how during imprisonment in dank, disgusting jail cells they would ask permission of the jailers to enter the cells of other prisoners, wash their wounds, clean the human waste from the floors, and care for them with love and kindness.

They would tell the prisoners about the love of Jesus Christ, who cared so much that he was willing to die for them . . . and then rose from the dead to give them new life. I wonder what it sounded like when a broken, dying prisoner prayed in a dungeon cell to ask for God's forgiveness and new life. I wonder what it sounded like when their prayers were heard by others, or maybe even their singing together in those dark, seemingly forgotten places? I'm sure the sounds filled the throne room of heaven.

Yes, serving can be messy at times, and maybe even a bit scary. The cross of Jesus Christ will always look messy, but it stands for a rescue mission he was willing to endure. Praise His name forever!

Chapter 18

You Are a Disciple of Jesus:
Heart, Mind, Body, Soul, and Spirit

Teaching Those You Disciple Who They Truly Are in Christ

You belong to Jesus!

Jesus is the King of kings. He is the Lord of lords. The author of the letter to the Hebrews states, "The Son is the radiance of God's glory and the exact representation of his being" (Hebrews 1:3). And according to John the apostle, Jesus is the One who created all things, both seen and unseen. He is the One celebrated in heaven right now. At this moment loud praises are being sung to him, while angels are flying around the throne of God exclaiming, "Worthy is the Lamb, who was slain, to receive power and wealth and wisdom and strength and honor and glory and praise!" And again, "To him who sits on the throne and to the Lamb be praise and honor and glory and power, for ever and ever!" (Revelation 5:12, 13). The adoration and celebration of Jesus Christ far exceed anything we could ever participate in during this life. Yet we are invited into this heavenly reality.

God the Father, through his Son Jesus Christ by the working of the Holy Spirit, has called you to walk with him in a close relationship, and he calls you his very own. The place you have been given is beyond description and comprehension. The apostle Paul writes that you have your citizenship in heaven (Philippians 3:20) and declares that you have been adopted into the family of God:

> *The spirit you received does not make you slaves, so that you live in fear again; rather, the Spirit you received brought about your adoption to sonship. And by him we cry, "Abba, Father." The Spirit himself testifies with our spirit that we are God's children. Now if we are children, then we are heirs—heirs of God and co-heirs with Christ, if indeed we share in his sufferings in order that we might share in his glory. (Romans 8:15–17)*

Peter comments that you are part of a royal line. "You are a chosen people, a royal priesthood, a holy nation, God's special possession, that you may declare the praises of him who called you out of the darkness into his wonderful light" (1 Peter 2:9). And Paul writes that you have the position of a saint. He refers to all believers in the Lord Jesus Christ when he addresses the Ephesian Christians as "the saints in Ephesus" (Ephesians 1:1).

The Greek word for saints is *hagios*, meaning "holy ones." What makes you holy? The blood of Jesus Christ. You have been redeemed and transformed, and you are a joint heir with Jesus Christ! You have a position with him as part of the family of God, and, in fact, he calls you his friend. If you are a man, the Scripture describes you as a son. If you are a woman, the Scripture identifies you as a daughter. In addition to all of this, you have been given, according to the apostle Paul, the mind of Christ (1 Corinthians 2:16), and, according to John, you have an anointing from God that leads you into all truth (1 John 2:20). The apostle Paul proclaims that you have the same spirit in you that raised Jesus Christ from the dead (Romans 6:10–11). Now that is power!

Paul wrote to the Corinthian church that his readers (and that includes you) have been given gifts and a place in the body of Christ that is supernatural, meaningful, and necessary for the body to function as it should (1 Corinthians 12:4–11). The body of Christ isn't complete without you.

When Jesus Christ died on the cross, he did so knowing that one day he would reach out to you personally to invite you into his kingdom, his heart, and his work. He chose you with a purpose and for a purpose. The greatest purpose is that you would know him intimately, as he knows you intimately. And his purposes for you abound beyond that to many incredible opportunities! Be assured of this: you are not alone. God declares, "Never will I leave you; never will I forsake you" (Hebrews 13:5). He is with you and in you through the presence and power of the Spirit of God.

You were designed and crafted by the creative genius of God himself. He says of you that you were fearfully and wonderfully made and that he has precious thoughts about you every day that outnumber the grains of sand on the earth! (Psalm 139:13–18). You were appointed to be alive at this particular time in history (Acts 17:26) to play a part in a grand plan that includes you with all of your strengths, weaknesses, flaws, and abilities. God wants to use your life to display his glory, but he first wants to show his glory to you and share his heart with you. Then he will flow through you naturally, as you have been designated by him to be the light of the world, a city on a hill that cannot be hidden, as Jesus declared in Matthew 5.

Our Father delights in you and is pleased to call you his own, and Jesus at this very moment is interceding for you before our Father (Romans 8:34). Even as Satan denounces you, Jesus confesses you as his own before our Father. There could be no greater witness and testimony than Jesus himself advocating for you by his blood and testimony about you!

So now, please understand that you were designed, purchased, given a royal position, and sent on a grand mission. While all of hell is bent on trying to dissuade you from receiving these truths, heaven has imparted angels, moved by the very Spirit of God with giftings and unending spiritual ability and endurance, so you can take part in the heavenly nature that God has given to you and walk with billions of brothers and sisters, who, like you, are finding their places in Jesus Christ and accepting his call.

These are truths about you that need to become intrinsic to your thinking. These are the truths you need to share and impart to those you walk with in discipleship. Together you walk as the church of the living God, firmly planted and built up more and more.

Earlier in this book I shared how I at times would leave my classroom for a break, walk to the staff bathroom, close the door, and speak aloud truths to myself to awaken my spirit and soul to God's promises and power in me. Once again I would like to offer you a declaration you can speak over yourself and over others that is based on God's promises to you. I invite you now to claim this as your own and speak it aloud:

"I am a child of the Living God. I have been born again by the Spirit of God who lives in me. Jesus Christ gave his life for me and has invited me into the family of God, the church, his body in this world. The blood Jesus shed on the cross freed me from all of the strongholds of the devil and his demons. There is no power that can hold me, no lie that can persuade me, for I am standing on the death, burial, and resurrection of my Lord and Savior Jesus Christ.

"The Spirit of God in me is the same that raised Jesus Christ from the dead. I have that same power living in me. I can do all things through Christ, who gives me strength. The weapons of my warfare are not of the flesh but are divinely powerful to demolish strongholds. I will take every thought captive to the obedience of Jesus Christ.

"I have an assignment from heaven, and I have been gifted by God to be a witness to others about Jesus's unconditional love. My mind is trained on God's Word, and my heart is filled with his agape love. My goal is to glorify my Father by living a life of virtue and honor to glorify the Lord Jesus here on earth. I am not afraid because God has not given me a spirit of fear but of power, love, and a sound mind. I do not fear the future or death, because God's perfect love has cast out fear.

"I have the sound mind God's Word says I have, for I have the mind of Christ. I am blessed with angels around me and billions of believers in the Lord Jesus Christ worldwide as my brothers and sisters. Together we are an army. I will stand on the truth, share the love of Jesus, and remain steadfast in the Word, praying through and worshiping my Savior. All praise to the One who loved me and gave himself for me. I am his, and he is mine! Lord, here I am—send me!"

Acknowledgments

If you have ever studied Paul's comments in Romans 16, then you know there were many brothers and sisters he thanked publicly. There are twenty-nine people named in Romans 16, as well as others who labored alongside them. I love the fact that Paul took time to tell people, "Hey—I want you to know who has been very special to me—these folks are rocks of faith in my journey!"

I'd like to take a few paragraphs to do something similar.

My wife is my greatest rock of faith. For almost forty years Anne has been a friend, a confidant, a prayer partner, and a ministry partner. We have traveled, worshiped, and served together, and we have lifted each other up even in situations and at times when there seemed to be no hope. I've written about her example, but our union goes much further than that. It is incredible to be married to the greatest example of motherhood and service I have ever witnessed. She is a caring counselor, a trusted friend to everyone who knows her. I love our journey together. Anne, you are amazing—as a partner, a mother, a challenging disciple, and a disciple-maker. Your commitment to Jesus is a testimony both here and in heaven. You are a continual challenger and my closest friend, and we continue to walk this road hand in hand.

My kids are rocks in my life. Jordan is my rock. He is wise and loyal, a patient counselor with people, and a true leader who has cared for me at times and has lifted me and let me know I am loved. Jordan, thank you for being my oldest and first son to walk with in discipleship. You are a wise and diligent leader. Your faithfulness is solid and secure. Holly, Jordan's wife, is also my rock. Holly's joy and love are readily felt, and her presence brightens the room when she is around.

My son Caleb is my rock. His exuberance and love for people are a healing balm. Laughter abounds when Caleb is around. If there is a trip to take or a place to talk, Caleb is in, and he makes it a blast. Caleb, you have been a constant companion in many situations. Your joy lights up our family. Thank you for your energy and passion. You are a ray of light. Caleb's wife, Courtney, is my rock. She is diligent and hard-working, with an endurance that doesn't quit. Courtney's heart is ten times the normal size.

My son Zach is my rock. He is a giant killer who is not afraid to take on any big assignments and who has a warrior's heart. Zach is multi-talented and creative in genius ways. Zach is curious and insightful. Zach, you have been awe inspiring in how you go after huge challenges and take down giants. You inspire and challenge me. Your creativity is extreme and brilliant. You are a man who inspires me to set high goals!

Alex is my rock. He is a man of quiet wisdom, creativity, and precision, and his ability with details astounds me. He is a steady force who offers timely quips that make me laugh! Alex, you are a challenge by the way you pursue excellence and bring gentlemanly maturity to every person and situation. Your creative leadership is awesome and your diligence is inspiring. Alex's wife, Victoria, is my rock of justice. She sees what should be and valiantly calls it out, challenging the status quo. Victoria is a challenger and leader.

My daughter, Lauren, is my rock, loving and serving Jesus and blessing everyone she encounters with joy and an incredible work ethic. Lauren is wise beyond her years and a Bible scholar who loves truth. Lauren, you are the princess of compassion, love, and joy. You change everyone around you, and I love watching you lead and bring joy to everyone. You are a life-changer.

Taylor is my rock. He is a gentle giant who will be joining the family soon and is a rock of stability and persistence. His dedication and love for people are profound.

I have been blessed to have had educators as rocks in my life, walking in faith with me. Their numbers include Mike, who is one of my closest friends, as well as Chris, Matt, Nate, Dave, Patsy, Shelby, Tracey, and Tracy. These brothers and sisters have blessed me in professionalism, faith, prayer, and through their support. They have encouraged and strengthened me in ways that only God could have provided. Their friendships have been a saving grace and inspiration to me.

There are many coaches who have been rocks along the way: Jack, Mike, Bruce, Brent, Brennan, Lee, Tom, John, Dave, and especially Jim. Thank you for being one of the first to share Jesus with me.

Many mentors have been rocks for me, beginning with my dad, the first person to explain the existence of God and cause me to think about him. My dad and mom together taught us to be moral and caring and to serve others. Your examples were indelibly imprinted over the years of trips and events, life and death, tears and laughter. The way you raised eight kids and regularly took a variety of other wrestlers with us wherever we went, even buying what they needed, demonstrated serving in a natural way.

Then there are Larry and Sharon, our spiritual mom and dad. You were the first to train us in being "sold out, the whole route," and you taught us to believe God's promises and to pray as though we expected to see God's hand move! Your prayers and counsel for us over the years encouraged us to be steady in Christ.

Nate, my wrestling mentor: you demonstrate talent, dedication, and a mind for the Word of God . . . and, dude, you can preach! Jeffrey—wow—I've already written it, but you have been the discipler of my life! To this day you are a rock and a hero to me. Dorr—you were the first to show me tears for a friend, an example that stirred me; to this day you remain a steady rock for me at all times. Loren—I would have to write another book to express my love and gratitude. Your example and your arms of love and acceptance have changed my life. I am a child at your feet.

The brothers and sisters I get to walk and go into battle with, you are my rocks! Mike, Tim and Shelly, Tony and Dawn, Brad and Kim, Tim and Gaye, Dave and Patty, Joyce, Mike and Sharon, Rob and Annette, Dave (Rod), Rob, Dan, Josh, Shelly, Doug, Billy, Doug, Kyle, Erik, Tom, Bill, Cam, Dave, Jeff, Jeff, Geoff, Walt, Roger, Scott, Nick, Charles, Todd, Chris, Brett, Tony, Keith, Traverse, Duane, Max, and Ron, you are for me a cloud of witnesses!

To those with whom I get to walk in discipleship—a lot or a little—I love each of you dearly: Reagan, Dan, Brett, Dave, Travis, Clay, Austin, Bryce, Erik, Kerry, Seth, Bryce, Travis, Brian, Connor, Andrew, Drew, Kennedy, Anna, Brian, Landon, Sam, Kiara, Sam, Scott and Suzie, and the myriad of brothers and sisters I get to text, email, and discuss life with, *thank you!* Your hunger and growth stir me!

Notes

1. The Science of the Brain (33) www.drleaf.com/blogs/news/you-are-not-a-victim-of-your-biology.
2. A and B type personality traits (33) www.medicalnewstoday.com/articles/type-a-vs-type-b#summary.
3. Number of Israelites in the desert: over two million souls (45) www.gotquestions.org/Israelites-exodus.html.
4. The Science of Giving Thanks: (55) www.health.harvard.edu/healthbeat/giving-thanks-can-make-you-happier.
5. Pleroo: Being filled with the Spirit of God (65) www.sermonindex.net/modules/articles/index.php?view=article&aid=34056#:~:text=Filled%20(4137)%20(pleroo),flood%2C%20to%20diffuse%20throughout%2C%20to.
6. Dead Sea and Sea of Galilee (83) www.google.com/search?q=picture+of+the+sea+of+galilee+and+the+dead+sea&rlz=1C5CHFA_enUS870US872&oq=picture+of+the+sea+of+galilee+and+the+dead+sea&aqs=chrome.0.69i59.12800j1j7&sourceid=chrome&i.
7. Yes, Virginia There is a Santa Claus: Library of Congress (99) guides. www.loc.gov/chronicling-america-yes-virginia.